ON THE RECORD

A Practical Guide to Crisis Communication
for Executives and Public Leaders

DIONNA SMITH

On the Record: A Practical Guide To Crisis Communication for Executives and Public Leaders

Published by On The Record Publishing
Atlanta, Georgia, USA
www.ontherecordpublishing.com

ISBN (Paperback): 979-8-9936069-0-3
ISBN (Hardcover): 979-8-9936069-1-0
ISBN (eBook): 979-8-9936069-2-7

Library of Congress Control Number (LCCN): 2025922669
Cover Photo: Nick Nelson
Cover Design: Payne Branding

Printed in the United States of America
First edition, **2026**
10 9 8 7 6 5 4 3 2 1

Disclaimer: The information in this book is provided for educational purposes and reflects the author's experience. It is not legal advice. Readers should consult qualified professionals regarding their specific circumstances.

Trademarks: All trademarks and product names are the property of their respective owners

Dedication

For the more than 600,000 Black women forced from the U.S. workforce. May history remember not only the loss of our labor, but the silence that followed.

TABLE OF CONTENTS

Epigraph

When leaders fail, it is rarely because they lack skill. It is because they underestimate the power of their silence. — On the Record

INTRODUCTION
When the Message Broke Before the Levee Did

"The storm broke the levees, but silence broke the people."

In August 2005, I was in Atlanta, home on maternity leave with my four-month-old son, Mark Alan. I was in my late twenties, learning the fragile rhythm of new motherhood: sleepless nights, soft breaths against my chest, the quiet awe of keeping someone alive.

I remember holding him in my arms, rocking in front of the television, when the news shifted from weather warnings to devastation.

My city, New Orleans, was drowning.

At first, it did not feel real. Hurricanes were familiar to us. We boarded windows, stocked up on food, and waited for storms to pass. But this one did not pass. It lingered. It tore. It swallowed everything.

The sound came first: the moan of wind bending steel, the crackle of reporters losing composure on live television, the pop of transformers exploding in the distance. Then came the images: rooftops barely visible above the waterline, families waving from attics, entire neighborhoods erased in real time.

I sat there clutching my baby, realizing that the world I came from was slipping away. With it came a grief I did not yet have language for. I mourned the city my son would never know: the second lines, the laughter spilling from porches, the smell of rain and red beans on Mondays, the sound of my grandmother humming on her front steps at dusk.

Years later, Mark Alan would move to New Orleans for college and become a musician. As if somewhere deep inside him, the rhythm of the city had already taken root, even then, when he was just a baby on my lap and we were both learning how to survive loss.

My grandmother, Mrs. Ida Smith Batiste, known as Ida Lee to those who loved her, had been evacuated to Texas just before the storm hit. We were grateful she was safe. But when she returned months later, the damage was almost unbearable.

Her roof was half gone. The walls sagged with moisture. Everything inside, furniture, photographs, heirlooms, carried the heavy smell of mildew. Her street stood quiet and unfamiliar, debris scattered where neighbors once gathered.

She stood on what remained of her stoop and whispered, almost to herself, "This don't even look like home no more."

Before Katrina, Ida Lee's kitchen had been the heart of our family. It was where truth lived. Where hard conversations happened before the world could have them first. She believed love meant telling the truth early and telling it fully.

"I don't ever want y'all hearing something in the streets that you didn't hear at home first," she used to say. "The purest form of love is truth."

When she called New Orleans "the city that care forgot," I once thought she meant resilience, our ability to laugh and live no matter what. Katrina taught me otherwise.

She meant neglect.

From Atlanta, I depended on leadership and the media to tell me what was happening. Instead, every voice contradicted the next. Officials hesitated. Messages splintered. And in the absence of clarity, speculation became gospel.

Black residents carrying groceries through floodwater were called looters.
White residents doing the same were called survivors.
Families searching for shelter were labeled refugees, strangers in their own land.

I remember shouting at the television, "We are not refugees in our own city."

It was the first time I fully understood how language could strip away dignity. How words, or the absence of them, could decide who is seen and who is erased.

The levees broke.
But the message broke first.

When it was finally safe to return, Ida Lee did what she had always done.

She cooked.

"Baby," she told me, "they can't find us on TV, but they can find me right here."

Her table became her command center. Her kitchen became a crisis response. People gathered to eat, to share information, to remember who they were before the water came.

In a world that had stopped listening, women like Ida Lee made themselves heard, not with microphones, but with presence.

Feed people food.
Feed them truth.
Feed them care until they remember they matter.

That was her leadership.

If Ida taught me how to speak truth, my grandmother Roxie taught me how to act on it.

Roxie lived in a corner of Mississippi most maps barely remembered. Her world ran on faith and fire, business and belief woven together. She organized, built, sold, fed, registered voters, and refused to let her people disappear.

Her porch was her press conference.
Her kitchen was her strategy room.
Her life was her message.

"See, baby," she once told me, shaping clay between her hands, "you gotta work it while it's soft. Wait too long, and it hardens before you can make it beautiful."

I did not know it then, but she was teaching me everything I would one day need to know about communication.

Timing matters.
Truth matters.
Courage matters.

Katrina was my first education in crisis.

It showed me what happens when leaders lose their voices, and what happens when ordinary people find theirs. It taught me that silence is not neutrality. It is neglect. That words can rescue or ruin. That leadership, at its core, is communication made visible.

I wrote this book because I believe communication is not a soft skill. It is a leadership responsibility. It is how trust is built, broken, and rebuilt in public view.

Woven through these pages are stories of crisis and clarity, failure and courage, leadership that rose, and leadership that retreated when it was needed most. Threaded through it all are the voices of my grandmothers, the women who taught me that truth is love in action.

Because storms will always come.

And when they do, the question is never whether people will talk.
It is whether leaders will speak with courage.

In the next chapter, we begin where every defining moment truly starts, before the statement, before the spotlight, before the crisis hits.

We begin with what you believe.

Because when pressure rises, leaders do not invent their message.
They return to what is already true.

And when the moment comes, your words should already know where to land.

PART I:
THE INNER WORK OF LEADERSHIP

Chapter 1
When the Pressure Hits

*"Pressure does not create leadership.
It reveals whether it was there to begin with."
— On the Record*

The moment rarely arrives with warning. It does not knock politely or wait until you feel ready. It does not ask whether the facts are confirmed, the advisors aligned, or the language approved. It arrives fractured, emotional, public, and urgent.

A video circulates before anyone understands what happened. A decision leaks before leadership has spoken. A tragedy occurs before the organization has words for grief. A leader is thrust into scrutiny with no time to rehearse. And suddenly, everything you say, or choose not to say, matters more than everything you have ever said before.

This is the moment where leadership is tested not by strategy, but by posture. Not by intention, but by presence. Not by what you know, but by how you show up when knowing is incomplete. This is the moment when communication stops being a function of leadership and becomes leadership itself.

Most leaders are not trained for this moment. They are trained to optimize, persuade, and perform. To lead with confidence, decisiveness, and control. They are rewarded for certainty, promoted for clarity, and praised for appearing unshaken.

But crisis does not reward performance. It exposes it. And when pressure hits, what is revealed is not your messaging skill. It is your capacity to steady others when you yourself are being tested.

The Lie We Tell Leaders

There is a quiet lie embedded in modern leadership culture.

It says that communication is something you do *after* decisions are made; that words are a delivery mechanism. A tool to manage reaction. A buffer between leadership and consequence.

This lie is tempting because it feels efficient.

It allows leaders to focus on action and outsource meaning. To believe that once the decision is final, the "right language" can be found. To assume that if a statement is polished enough, the moment will soften.

But under pressure, this lie collapses.

Because people do not experience leadership in sequence. They experience it simultaneously.

They experience:

- What you do
- What you say
- When you say it
- How you say it
- And whether you stay visible afterward

When those elements are misaligned, trust fractures, sometimes permanently.

This is why leaders who make the *same* decision can experience wildly different outcomes. One stabilizes their organization. Another triggers chaos. One is remembered as steady. Another as evasive or cold.

The difference is not intelligence.
It is not intent.
It is not even the decision itself.

It is communication under pressure.

What Pressure Reveals

Pressure does not make leaders reckless. It reveals what they rely on when certainty disappears.

Some rely on silence, hoping time will protect them. Others rely on defensiveness, mistaking explanation for leadership. Some turn to legal language, confusing protection with trust. Others perform, believing confidence will substitute for clarity.

And some, more rarely, rely on discipline.

They slow themselves before the moment accelerates. They name what people are feeling before explaining policy. They speak facts carefully, without weaponizing them. They remain present long after the attention fades.

These leaders are not fearless. They are regulated. And regulation, not confidence, is what steadies people when the ground is moving.

My Education Was Not Academic

I did not learn this in theory. I learned it watching systems fail in real time.

I learned it during Hurricane Katrina, when silence from those in power became its own form of violence. People were not only stranded physically, but narratively, unseen, unnamed, and unacknowledged. Delay and deflection multiplied harm instead of containing it.

I learned it years later inside corporate crisis rooms during COVID, when leaders were forced to speak without answers and reassure without certainty. Every email carried fear, and every pause felt ominous. Employees were not asking for perfection, but for honesty and presence.

I learned it again during the moral reckoning that followed the murder of George Floyd, when neutrality collapsed and silence was interpreted as alignment. Leaders discovered, often too late, that carefully worded statements mean nothing if they are not backed by courage.

And I learned it most profoundly in public service, where communication is no longer reputational, it is lived. Words affect safety, access, and dignity. Messaging failures are not abstract. They are felt in communities that cannot opt out.

Across all of these moments, one truth repeated itself relentlessly.

Crisis does not destroy trust.
Avoidance does.

Why Leaders Fail When It Matters Most

Most leadership failures in crisis are not moral failures. They are timing failures.

Leaders wait too long to acknowledge harm. They explain before they recognize. They speak once and disappear. They treat accountability as an event instead of a posture. And when leaders disappear, fear fills the void.

People do not expect leaders to have all the answers. They expect leaders to stay present while answers are found. When that expectation is violated, credibility erodes, even if the eventual explanation is sound.

This is why leadership communication cannot be improvised. It must be disciplined.

The Discovery of C.A.L.M.

C.A.L.M. was not created as a framework. It was discovered as a pattern.

After years of watching what steadied organizations and what destabilized them, I noticed the same sequence emerge again and again in moments that held. Leaders who survived pressure consistently did four things, in order.

They centered themselves before responding. They acknowledged impact before explaining facts. They led with facts carefully, sequencing truth to stabilize rather than defend. They modeled accountability through sustained presence, not performative statements.

When leaders followed this sequence, even imperfectly, panic slowed. Trust bent without breaking. Meaning stabilized. When they did not, even flawless messaging failed.

C.A.L.M. is not about tone, style, or sounding reassuring. It is about regulating leadership so others can breathe.

This Is Not a Communications Book

Let me be clear about what this book is not. It is not about branding, spin, winning the news cycle, or crafting the perfect statement.

This is a leadership book for moments when leadership is most visible and most vulnerable. It is for executives, public officials, nonprofit leaders, and political figures who understand that authority is not proven in calm seasons, but in storms. It is for leaders who know that their words will outlive the moment in which they are spoken.

And it is for those willing to accept this truth.

Your voice is not accidental.
Your silence is not neutral.
And when pressure hits, how you communicate becomes who you are.

The Threshold

This chapter is the threshold.

Everything that follows will build on one central question:

Who are you when certainty disappears?

The chapters ahead will walk through how leaders:

- Center themselves under pressure
- Acknowledge harm without legal panic or defensiveness
- Use facts as anchors, not shields
- Model accountability when retreat would be easier
- Own the story before it owns them
- Speak for institutions, not just themselves
- Lead without certainty—and still be trusted

But before any of that matters, this must be settled:

Communication is not something you add to leadership.

It *is* leadership.

And when it matters most, it is the difference between chaos and calm.

Chapter 2
Finding Your Voice

"If not you, then who?"
— Grandma Ida

The kitchen on Plum Street was more than a room with an oven and a table. It was a gathering place, a classroom, and a pulpit. My grandmother Ida cooked there, cleaned there, talked on the phone there, and gathered family and neighbors there. The air was always heavy with the smell of gumbo or fried catfish, and somewhere down the block, music drifted through the heat.

I sat cross-legged on the steps just outside the kitchen door, listening through the screen, watching, absorbing. Long before I had language for leadership, I was learning what it looked like.

People did not come to Ida because she was loud. They came because she was clear. Neighbors passed by not just to say hello, but to ask for counsel about a lost job, a sick child, a marriage in trouble, an argument that needed mending. Ida listened longer than she spoke. And when she did speak, her words carried weight.

She understood something many leaders never learn. Words are never neutral. They either stabilize a moment or destabilize it.

By the time I was eight, I knew everybody's business on the block and more than a few family secrets. I asked too many clarifying questions, offered unsolicited advice to grown folks, and repeated things I should not have heard. Ida would look at me over her glasses and say, "Baby, everything you hear ain't meant for you to repeat."

What she was teaching me was discernment. Listening is not the same as speaking. Speaking is not the same as leadership. Even then, I was learning that voice is not just expression. It is responsibility.

Though I spent my summers sweating in the Mississippi heat with Grandma Roxie, the rest of the year belonged to Ida. Every afternoon after school, I settled into her living room, watched her stories, ate sandwiches, and helped stir pots of dinner that always smelled like home. Ida's voice carried both melody and command. She rarely raised it. She did not need to.

The two of them, my grandmothers, balanced me like twin pillars. Roxie gave me the will to act. Ida gave me the courage to speak.

I did not know then that their lessons would one day guide me through boardrooms, press conferences, and moments when entire communities would look for clarity in chaos. I only knew this. My grandmothers never confused humility with silence.

The Sound of Silence

Before you can lead with your voice, you must learn to hear it. Ida understood that intuitively. She used to say, "Don't just listen to what people say. Listen to what they don't say."

I did not fully understand what she meant until years later, in the most devastating way imaginable.

I was twenty-nine when the levees broke.

Hurricane Katrina did not just destroy homes. It exposed the catastrophic consequences of leadership that was delayed, diluted, and detached. Phones went unanswered. Messages conflicted. Responsibility passed from one level of government to another while people waited on rooftops.

The images are burned into my memory. The Superdome filled with despair. Families separated and mislabeled as refugees in their own country. A city reduced to a cautionary tale instead of a human tragedy.

What haunted me most was not the water. It was the absence of a clear, compassionate voice.

Leaders spoke too late, too cautiously, or not at all. Statements sounded procedural when people needed humanity. The gap between reality and response widened, and in that gap, trust drowned.

That was my first lesson in crisis communication, though I did not yet have the vocabulary for it. I only understood this: when leaders fail to speak with clarity and care, silence becomes harmful.

Case Study of Failure

Katrina and the Cost of Delayed Voice

Hurricane Katrina was not a communication failure because leaders lacked information. It was a failure because they lacked voice clarity when urgency demanded it.

In August 2005, as Katrina approached the Gulf Coast, meteorologists issued increasingly dire warnings. Emergency management officials had data. Forecasts were clear. The danger was real and imminent. And yet leadership communication lagged behind the reality on the ground.

Evacuation orders were inconsistent and late. Messaging varied by jurisdiction. Responsibility was fragmented between city, state, and federal leadership, each waiting for the other to move first. Press conferences were held, but the language was procedural instead of urgent. People heard the term "mandatory evacuation" without the emotional gravity required to compel action.

When the levees broke, communication collapsed entirely.

Phones went unanswered. Information contradicted itself. Leaders appeared on television detached from the suffering unfolding in real time. People stranded on rooftops did not hear reassurance. They heard confusion. Families in the Superdome did not hear clarity. They heard delay.

The most devastating aspect of Katrina was not just the storm itself. It was the absence of a steady, human voice when people needed it most.

Leadership did not fail because it spoke incorrectly. It failed because it did not speak clearly enough, early enough, or humanly enough.

The silence and fragmentation created a story that hardened quickly. That leadership was disconnected. That help was not coming. That people had been abandoned. And once that story took hold, no amount of explanation could undo the damage.

Lesson for leaders: Silence is not neutral in crisis. It becomes a message of neglect. Voice is not only about delivering information. It is about conveying urgency, care, and responsibility at the same time.

When leaders delay speaking because they fear being wrong, they often become irrelevant. When they speak without humanity, they become untrustworthy.

Katrina teaches this hard truth. When leaders do not claim their voice, chaos claims it for them.

When Performance Replaces Presence

We live in a world that rewards immediacy and volume. Everyone is expected to respond instantly. Yet in high-stakes moments, speed without grounding creates damage.

I have watched leaders speak quickly and say nothing. I have watched others stay silent and say everything.

Some hide behind corporate language so polished it removes all humanity. Others overshare in the name of authenticity, confusing emotional exposure with leadership.

Both are performances.

Performance seeks safety. Presence creates trust.

The leaders who communicate most effectively under pressure are not the most eloquent. They are the most aligned. They know what they believe before the room demands answers.

That is what Ida meant by "If not you, then who?"

She was not telling me to talk more. She was telling me to talk truer.

My Turning Point

Speaking When Silence Felt Safer

In 2020, I stepped into the role of Head of Diversity, Equity, and Inclusion at a global technology company at precisely the wrong time and exactly the right one.

America was unraveling.

A once-in-a-century pandemic had stripped away the illusion that we were all experiencing the same storm. Essential workers were praised while being sacrificed. Black and brown communities were dying at higher rates. Entire industries collapsed overnight. People worked from kitchen tables, bedrooms, and cars, trying to hold together jobs and families with the same exhausted hands.

Then came the killings that removed any remaining cover from the lie of progress. George Floyd. Breonna Taylor. Ahmaud Arbery. Three names. Three lives. Three moments that forced a reckoning no corporate statement, carefully worded press release, or diversity pledge could outrun.

The world did not just ask organizations where they stood. It demanded to know who they were.

That was when my phone stopped behaving like a phone and became something else entirely. It became an emergency line.

Texts came first, then emails, then calendar invitations marked urgent and confidential. My days blurred into back-to-back calls with executives whose voices sounded unfamiliar even to themselves. Some were angry. Some were afraid. Some were genuinely heartbroken. Most were unprepared.

They asked the same question in different ways. Should we speak now or wait. What if we say the wrong thing. What if we make it worse.

What they were really asking was simpler and harder. What if we are exposed.

I heard the tension beneath their words. These were leaders fluent in metrics and strategy. They could read balance sheets and growth projections without breaking a sweat. They had navigated mergers, acquisitions, product failures, and market volatility. But this moment felt different.

This was not about performance. It was about identity. And identity cannot be outsourced.

What I saw was not malice. It was inexperience. Leaders rewarded for decisiveness in operational crises, but untrained in humanity. Leaders who had never been taught how to lead when the crisis was moral, emotional, and deeply personal.

They were terrified of saying the wrong thing, so they said nothing. Or worse, they waited. They convened committees. They asked legal to review language. They debated tone while employees watched the news and wondered whether their employers saw them as human beings or liabilities.

Every delay widened the gap between leadership and trust. Every hour of silence spoke louder than any statement that would come later.

As I listened, something inside me kept returning to a memory I could not shake. Katrina. I remembered what it felt like to watch leaders hesitate while people drowned. I remembered the way silence sounded like abandonment. I remembered how procedural language landed like indifference.

And I knew, with a clarity that surprised even me, that silence could not be the response again. Not this time.

The irony was that my own body was in crisis as well. I was on bed rest, recovering from postpartum preeclampsia. My blood pressure had spiked dangerously after giving birth. My body was fragile in ways I had never experienced before. Survival felt close, intimate, and non-negotiable.

My newborn son slept beside me as I worked. I rocked him with one arm and muted myself on Zoom calls when he cried. I nursed between strategy sessions. I adjusted talking points while monitoring my own recovery.

The juxtaposition was relentless. By day, I coached CEOs on how to acknowledge racial trauma without defensiveness. By night, I held my baby and wondered what kind of world he was being born into.

I explained to leaders why "we value diversity" sounded hollow in a moment of bloodshed. I helped them replace corporate distance with human language. I slowed them down when they wanted to rush to facts while their people were drowning in grief.

Over and over, I said some version of the same thing. You do not need the perfect words. You need the honest ones. You do not need to explain everything. You need to acknowledge what is happening. You do not need certainty. You need courage.

There were moments when silence would have been easier for me, too. Exhaustion made it tempting to retreat, to protect myself, to say less. The emotional labor of carrying both professional responsibility and personal fear felt overwhelming.

But every time I considered pulling back, I thought about the cost of silence I had already witnessed in my lifetime.

And I chose to speak.

Those weeks were heavy, not because the work was hard, but because it mattered. Because every word landed somewhere real. Because leaders were not just shaping statements. They were shaping whether people felt seen or erased.

And somewhere in that exhaustion, something permanent clarified for me.

Honest communication is not risky. Avoidance is.

Silence does not protect leaders from scrutiny. It delays accountability and deepens distrust. Carefully avoiding discomfort does not prevent damage. It compounds it.

That was the turning point.

Not just in my career, but in my understanding of leadership itself.

Finding your voice is not about confidence. It is about responsibility. And when silence feels safer, that is often the moment your voice is needed most.

Case Study of Success

Jacinda Ardern and the Christchurch Response

In March 2019, New Zealand experienced one of the most horrific acts of violence in its history. A gunman attacked two mosques in Christchurch, killing 51 people and injuring dozens more. The nation was stunned. Grief spread quickly, and fear followed close behind.

Within hours, Prime Minister **Jacinda Ardern** addressed the country. She did not hide behind policy language. She did not wait for perfect facts. She did not center herself. She centered the people.

Her first public words acknowledged pain directly: "They are us." With that single phrase, she reframed the moment. The victims were not outsiders. They were part of the national "we." Her tone was calm, firm, and unmistakably human. She named the grief. She rejected the ideology behind the violence without amplifying it. She refused to say the attacker's name, explaining later that she would not give him notoriety.

Then she acted.

Within weeks, New Zealand passed sweeping gun reform legislation. Ardern stood before Parliament wearing a headscarf in solidarity with the Muslim community. She met with families privately. She returned again and again to the same message of empathy, accountability, and unity.

This was not performative empathy. It was aligned leadership. Her voice matched her actions. Her actions reinforced her words. Because of that alignment, trust deepened rather than fractured.

Lesson for leaders: Finding your voice is not about charisma. It is about conviction under pressure. Ardern's clarity came from values defined before the crisis arrived. She did not invent a response. She revealed who she already was.

Clarity does not require volume. Empathy does not weaken authority. Alignment builds trust faster than perfection ever could.

Finding Your Voice in the Real World

Finding your voice does not guarantee universal approval. In fact, clarity often invites resistance. But leadership is not about consensus. It is about alignment.

When leaders speak with conviction, they help people locate themselves in the moment. They reduce confusion. They stabilize meaning. They make it possible for others to act. When leaders speak vaguely, defensively, or too late, they invite speculation and fracture. They create space for fear to fill what clarity should have held.

This is why voice matters before strategy. This is why alignment matters before optics.

Voice Readiness

Before you can lead with calm, you must understand your relationship to voice. Under pressure, do you default to silence? Do you over-explain when nervous? Do you delay until the moment passes? Do you intellectualize to avoid emotion? Do you seek the safest sentence instead of the truest one?

These patterns are not just communication habits. They are leadership habits.

Finding your voice is not about becoming someone else. It is about recognizing who you become under pressure and deciding, in advance, who you intend to be.

A Return to the Porch

When I think about the leaders I admire most, my grandmothers, Jacinda Ardern, and those who spoke truth when silence felt safer, I see the same thread.

Clarity rooted in care.

When I prepare leaders for high-stakes moments, I think of Ida's porch. The smell of evening rain. Her steady voice saying, "Baby, if not you, then who?"

Leadership is not volume. It is virtue.

Finding your voice is the beginning. Learning to steady it is the work.

In the next chapter, we move inward. We will explore how leaders center themselves before they speak, because calm is not a personality trait. It is a practiced discipline.

Finding your voice is not the finish line. It is the threshold.

Voice without grounding can become reaction.
Voice without clarity can become noise.
Voice without discipline can become harm.

When pressure arrives, you will not rise to the occasion.

You will default to your discipline.

And calm is trained.

PART II: COMMUNICATING WITH C.A.L.M.

Chapter 3
Centering Yourself Before the Storm

"If you cannot regulate yourself, you will escalate the moment."
— *On the Record*

Chapter 2 ends with a truth most leaders learn too late: when pressure arrives, you will not rise to the occasion. You will default to your discipline. That is why this chapter comes next.

Before a leader speaks, something else always speaks first. It is not the message, the facts, or the strategy. It is the body.

The breath shortens. The jaw tightens. The shoulders climb toward the ears. The eyes scan the room for threat instead of connection. In high-stakes moments, people are not listening first for words. They are reading signals. They are assessing whether the person in front of them is steady enough to be trusted with what comes next.

Long before your message reaches them, your nervous system has already introduced you.

This is why leaders lose credibility before they ever open their mouths, and why centering yourself is not a soft skill or a wellness trend. It is a leadership discipline, a prerequisite, and a dividing line between leaders who stabilize moments and leaders who unknowingly escalate them.

Where I First Learned Emotional Control

I spent many summers at the bottom of a dirt road in Meridian, Mississippi, where the nights grew so dark they forced you to listen. Cicadas hummed in the trees. Frogs croaked near the pond. When rain hit the tin roof of my great-grandparents' house, each drop became percussion.

That house belonged to Noel and Lena Bell, Big Mama to everyone who knew her. The porch sagged under decades of use. The walls sighed with age. The air smelled like old wood, hot grease, and patience earned the hard way.

Some of the most formative lessons did not happen inside that house. They happened down the road on Sundays at Shiloh Baptist Church.

Shiloh sat at the edge of the cemetery, surrounded by headstones that carried names older than freedom. Some leaned, weathered and worn, the letters barely visible but still legible to those who knew how to look. Inside the church, time slowed. Services lasted hours. No one rushed the spirit. No one rushed the word.

There was rhythm and restraint, pauses long enough to breathe.

The preacher never began by shouting. He began by settling the room. The choir did not sing to perform. They sang to prepare. Call and response was not noise. It was regulation, a collective slowing of breath, heart rate, and attention.

Long before I understood neuroscience, leadership psychology, or crisis communication, I was watching emotional containment in action. I was watching how a room full of people learned to move together, to hold grief without being consumed by it, to make space for truth to land without shattering them.

What the church taught me, quietly and repeatedly, was this: before people can hear truth, they must feel safe enough to receive it. That safety does not come from volume or urgency. It comes from control.

Why Leaders Escalate the Moment Without Realizing It

Most leaders believe crisis requires immediacy. Say something. Say it now. Fill the silence.

Silence feels dangerous. It feels like abdication and loss of control. So leaders rush to speak, believing speed signals authority. But urgency without regulation is not leadership. It is acceleration.

I have watched leaders unravel credibility in seconds, not because they lacked intelligence or preparation, but because their internal state leaked into the room. Their bodies spoke panic before their words could convey competence.

Voices tightened. Pacing accelerated. Answers arrived before the question had finished forming. Even when the facts were correct, the delivery betrayed instability. People responded not to the content, but to the energy behind it.

When leaders are not centered, their tone sharpens, their language becomes defensive or abstract, and their presence feels brittle. People may nod and listen politely, but internally, trust begins to erode.

People do not argue with facts first. They react to energy. This is why calm is not cosmetic. It is operational.

The Body Always Goes First

High-stakes communication is physiological before it is intellectual. When pressure hits, the nervous system decides whether you are safe before the mind decides what to say. If your body is in fight or flight, your words will follow. That is not a character flaw. It is biology.

Under stress, leaders often do predictable things. They over-explain to regain control. They interrupt to assert dominance. They retreat into jargon to avoid emotion. They rush toward resolution to escape discomfort.

These behaviors are not personality traits. They are stress responses.

Centering yourself is the act of interrupting those responses long enough to regain choice. Choice of tone, pace, language, and leadership.

Without centering, leaders do not choose their response.

They default to it.

What Centering Actually Requires

Centering is often misunderstood. It is not detachment. It is not emotional suppression. It is not pretending everything is fine.

Centering is the ability to stay with yourself when pressure tries to pull you away.

It is the moment you notice your breath becoming shallow, your chest tightening, your impulse to defend or deflect rising, and you pause.

Not to disappear. Not to delay indefinitely. But to anchor.

That pause is where leadership begins.

Because once you are centered, you are no longer reacting to the room.

You are shaping it.

Why Calm Is Read as Competence

People trust leaders who appear anchored. Not because they have all the answers, but because they are not undone by uncertainty. In moments of crisis, credibility does not come from certainty.

It comes from composure.

I have watched rooms de-escalate simply because a leader slowed their pace. I have seen anger soften when someone acknowledged the weight of the moment without rushing to solve it. I have watched fear give way to focus when a leader's voice remained steady while everything else felt unstable.

This is not accidental. Humans mirror emotional cues. When a leader remains grounded, it gives others permission to regulate themselves as well. Calm spreads faster than panic, but only if someone introduces it first.

Leadership communication is not about overpowering emotion.

It is about containing it.

The Discipline of Restraint

One of the hardest skills for high-performing leaders to learn is restraint. You are trained to act, to solve, to move quickly. But leadership communication requires a different discipline: knowing when you are not yet ready to speak.

Centering yourself means recognizing when your emotions are driving your message, when urgency is rooted in fear of perception, and when the desire to speak is about control rather than clarity. Restraint is not silence. It is preparation. It is the difference between reacting to pressure and responding to reality.

A Real-World Moment

The Press Conference That Could Have Gone Sideways

I once worked with a senior leader preparing for a press conference following a public failure. The facts were clear. The corrective actions were already underway. On paper, the response was sound.

But the leader was not.

Minutes before stepping to the podium, his breathing was shallow, his speech rapid, his posture rigid. He wanted to rush through the statement and get it over with.

We paused. Not for optics, but for regulation.

He slowed his breathing. He grounded his stance. He stopped trying to escape the weight of the moment and allowed himself to carry it. When he spoke, the words were nearly identical to the original draft.

But the impact was completely different.

The room softened. Questions were firm but fair. Coverage focused on accountability instead of defensiveness. The difference was not messaging. It was centering.

When Calm Protects a Mission

Nonprofit leaders face a unique kind of pressure because their credibility is not just reputational. It is relational. It is moral. It is tied to donors, communities, clients, staff, and the people the mission exists to serve.

Consider a moment familiar across many mission-driven organizations. A nonprofit is accused publicly of mishandling funds or of internal harm that contradicts its values. Social media moves faster than the facts. A major donor calls. A board member panics. Staff members are scared. Community partners want answers immediately. Reporters begin emailing within hours.

This is the moment when many nonprofit leaders try to sound official instead of human. They hide behind process. They rush to reassure. They default to language designed to reduce legal exposure, even if it increases emotional damage.

But I have seen the opposite.

I have seen a nonprofit executive lead with centering first. She walked into the room and did not begin with statements. She began with breath. She named what was true internally before anything went public: "We are triggered. We are afraid. We are also responsible."

She reduced the noise. She clarified roles. She stabilized the team so they could think.

Then she prepared to speak, not from panic or defensiveness, but from discipline. When she addressed staff, she did not rush into explanation. She acknowledged the weight of the accusation and the fear it created. When she addressed external stakeholders, she did not over-promise or spin. She committed to a transparent process and explained what accountability would look like, including how and when people would hear from the organization again.

What made her effective was not that she had perfect answers on day one. It was that she was steady enough to carry uncertainty without disappearing.

That steadiness protected the mission. It protected staff morale. It protected public trust. It prevented the crisis from turning into collapse.

And it started with a decision most leaders skip. Center first.

How Leaders Lose Trust Before They Mean To

Many communications failures do not fail because the message was wrong. They fail because the leader was unregulated.

You can hear it in apologies that sound rushed. You can see it in press conferences where shoulders tense and eyes dart. You can feel it in statements that try to close a moment before it has been acknowledged. When leaders skip centering, empathy sounds performative, facts feel dismissive, and accountability feels transactional.

People sense the disconnect immediately. You cannot steady others if you are not steady yourself.

Centering as a Leadership Habit

The most effective leaders do not wait for crisis to practice calm. They build it in advance.

They understand their stress patterns. They recognize what triggers defensiveness. They know how fear shows up in their bodies and speech. They practice slowing down before pressure forces them to.

This self-awareness is not introspection for its own sake. It is preparation. Because when the moment comes, and it always does, you will not invent composure.

You will return to what you have practiced.

That is why centering is not a one-time act. It is a habit.

The Cost of Skipping This Step

When leaders skip centering, everything that follows suffers.

Acknowledgment sounds hollow. Facts sound cold. Accountability feels forced.

This is why so many public apologies fail. The words are right, but the delivery is wrong. The leader has not steadied themselves, so nothing they say can steady others.

You cannot borrow calm.

You must generate it.

Why This Step Comes First

Everything that follows in leadership communication depends on this step.

You cannot acknowledge emotion authentically if you are overwhelmed by your own. You cannot lead with facts if your delivery amplifies fear. You cannot model accountability if your body signals avoidance.

Centering yourself is not optional.

It is the ground on which every other skill stands.

A Return to the Church

When I think back to Shiloh Baptist Church, I realize now that what I witnessed was not performance.

It was regulation.

The choir did not rush the song. The preacher did not rush the message. The congregation did not rush the response. They moved together, breath by breath, creating space for truth to land.

That is leadership.

Not volume. Not urgency. Not dominance.

Control in service of care.

Preparing for the Next Movement

Centering yourself does not end the work. It begins it.

Once you are grounded, you must turn outward toward the people in front of you, toward their fear, their anger, their grief. That requires a different discipline: acknowledging emotion without surrendering authority.

In the next chapter, we will explore how leaders name what people are feeling without collapsing into it or avoiding it altogether, and why this step often determines whether trust grows or fractures.

Because calm is not silence.

It is readiness.

And readiness is what allows your words to carry weight when they matter most.

Chapter 4
Acknowledging Emotion Without Losing Authority

How leaders name fear, anger, and grief without surrendering leadership

**"People do not need to be calmed.
They need to be understood."**
— On the Record

The Most Skipped Step in Leadership Communication

There is a moment in every crisis when facts are still forming, systems are still adjusting, and people are already emotional. This is the moment most leaders rush through. They hurry to explain, reassure, and sound competent. In doing so, they skip the most essential leadership task of all: acknowledging what people are feeling before asking them to understand anything else.

Emotion is not a distraction from leadership communication. It is the entry point. Until fear, anger, grief, or confusion is named, facts do not land. Accountability does not register. Authority does not feel credible. Leaders may be heard, but they are not trusted.

Acknowledgment is not weakness. It is sequencing. Leaders who fail to master this step do not lose credibility because they are wrong. They lose it because they are misaligned with the moment they are speaking into.

Why Acknowledgment Must Come Before Explanation

Most leadership breakdowns in crisis happen because leaders explain too soon. They move to logic while people are still afraid, to justification while people are still grieving, and to solutions while people are still asking a quieter question: Do you see me?

When leaders skip acknowledgment, they create a gap between message and reality. In that gap, distrust grows.

Acknowledgment does not mean agreement, apology, or surrender. It means recognition.

It sounds like this: "We understand why this feels frightening." "We know this decision hurts." "We recognize the anger and confusion this has caused." "We know many of you are carrying fear right now."

Those statements do not weaken authority. They stabilize the room.

What People Need Before They Can Hear You

In high-stakes moments, people process information in a predictable order. First, they scan for safety. Then they look for meaning. Only after that do they absorb details.

Most leaders try to start with details. That is backwards.

When you start with details while people are still scanning for safety, your message sounds like distance, even if it is true.

You can deliver accurate information and still fail the moment if you deliver it out of sequence.

Acknowledgment tells people three things at once:

1. You are paying attention.
2. You understand impact, not just facts.
3. You are steady enough to hold what they are feeling without running from it.

That is authority.

Not dominance. Not volume. Not certainty. Steadiness.

The Lie Leaders Tell Themselves

Leaders often believe this: "If I acknowledge emotion, I will make it worse," or, "If I acknowledge emotion, I will lose control."

The opposite is usually true.

Emotion that is acknowledged tends to settle. Emotion that is ignored tends to intensify. Emotion that is minimized tends to erupt. People do not escalate because you named what they feel. They escalate because they believe you are trying to bypass it.

Acknowledgment is containment. It says, I see this, and I am not overwhelmed by it. That signal matters more than any policy explanation.

The Difference Between Acknowledgment and Apology

This is where leaders often get stuck. They fear that naming emotion equals admitting wrongdoing. It does not.

Acknowledgment is about impact. Apology is about responsibility. Sometimes both are needed. Often, in early moments, only one is appropriate.

You can acknowledge fear without conceding fault. You can acknowledge anger without validating every accusation. You can acknowledge grief without having every detail confirmed.

Leaders who understand this stop treating emotion like a legal threat and start treating it like what it is: a reality.

Personal Narrative

Leading Through Loss Without Losing Humanity

I learned the discipline of acknowledgment most sharply while helping leaders communicate through a large-scale corporate layoff.

The decision itself had already been made. Market conditions had shifted. Revenue forecasts tightened. Jobs were going to be eliminated, many of them held by people who had given years of loyalty and effort to the organization.

The leaders were prepared with numbers. They had spreadsheets, timelines, and legal language. What they were not prepared for was the emotional impact.

Remote employees logged on from kitchen tables. Parents sat just off camera with children home from school. Employees already carrying the fatigue of the pandemic were now being told their livelihoods were ending through a screen.

The instinct from leadership was to explain immediately. Why the decision was necessary. Why it was unavoidable. Why it was not personal.

But explanation was not what people needed first.

People needed acknowledgment. They needed someone to say, plainly and without defensiveness: "We know this is painful." "We know this feels sudden." "We know this affects more than just your job." "We know you are worried about what comes next."

When leaders resisted that step, the reaction was swift. Chat windows filled with anger. Emails turned sharp. Trust evaporated in real time.

But when leaders slowed down and acknowledged emotion first, something changed. People still grieved. They still disagreed. They were still hurt. But they listened.

Acknowledgment did not erase the loss. It gave people dignity inside it.

That moment clarified something essential. Leaders do not lose authority by naming pain. They lose authority by pretending it is not there.

What Acknowledgment Sounds Like in Practice

Many leaders ask, "Okay, but what do I actually say?"

Here is what effective acknowledgment does in one or two sentences:

- **Names the emotional reality** without inflaming it.
- **Signals understanding** without over-promising.
- **Creates space** before facts arrive.

A strong acknowledgment sentence usually includes three ingredients:

1. **Awareness**
   "We are aware of what happened."

"We have seen the video."
"We know this news is landing hard."

2. **Impact**
"We understand why this is concerning."
"We recognize this is painful."
"We know this brings fear, frustration, and questions."

3. **Presence**
"We are here."
"We will keep you informed."
"We are taking this seriously and will communicate as we learn more."

That is enough to stabilize the room.

Not forever. But long enough to lead.

The Trap of "Calming" People

One of the most common leadership missteps is trying to calm people instead of trying to understand them.

Leaders say:

"Everyone just needs to calm down."
"There is no reason to panic."
"This is being blown out of proportion."
"Let's be rational."

These phrases do not calm people.

They insult them.

They communicate: your reaction is inconvenient.

And when people feel judged for their emotion, they stop trusting your message and start challenging your motive.

People do not want to be managed emotionally.

They want to be respected.

The Five Most Common Acknowledgment Mistakes

Even leaders who try to acknowledge emotion often do it in ways that backfire. Here are the patterns to avoid:

1. Minimizing
"I know this is upsetting, but…"
"While this is unfortunate…"
"At the end of the day…"

Translation: your emotion is a speed bump.

2. Performing empathy
"We hear you" with no specificity.
"Your concerns matter" with no follow-through.

Translation: we are checking a box.

3. Talking past the moment
Leaders deliver a speech as if the audience is not emotional.

Translation: I prepared a script, not a response.

4. Over-identifying
"I know exactly how you feel."
"This hurts me more than anyone."

Translation: I am centering myself.

5. Rushing to solutions
"Here is what we are doing" before naming what people are experiencing.

Translation: I want this to be over.

Acknowledgment fails when it sounds like a technique instead of a posture.

Case Study: Failure to Acknowledge Emotion

When the Memo Becomes the Story

In the early months of the pandemic, one global company announced widespread layoffs through a brief, impersonal memo. The message focused almost entirely on financial necessity. It explained market pressures, operational realities, and the need to protect long-term viability.

What it did not do was acknowledge the human cost.

There was no recognition of fear, no acknowledgment of grief, and no language suggesting leaders understood what this meant for the people reading it.

The reaction was immediate. Employees flooded social media with stories of being blindsided. Journalists picked up on the emotional disconnect. Former employees described feeling discarded, not separated.

The company was factually correct, but emotionally absent. And that absence became the story.

What failed here was not strategy. It was sequencing. Leaders moved to explanation before recognition. They treated emotion as an inconvenience instead of a reality. The result was reputational damage far beyond the layoffs themselves.

Case Study: Acknowledgment Done Well

When the CEO Earns the Right to Explain

Contrast that with another organization facing similar circumstances. This leadership team began their communication differently.

Before any explanation of financial pressures, the CEO spoke directly to emotion. "I know this news is frightening. I know many of you are worried about what this means for your families. I want to acknowledge the shock and anger some of you may be feeling."

Only after naming those emotions did the leader explain the decision.

The facts were no softer. The outcome was no less painful. But the response was markedly different. Employees expressed sadness, not outrage. Media coverage focused on transparency instead of cruelty. Even those leaving the organization described feeling respected, not erased.

Acknowledgment did not change the decision. It changed the experience.

Why Leaders Struggle With This Step

Leaders skip acknowledgment for predictable reasons. They fear it will escalate emotion. They fear it will create liability. They fear they will not know what to do next.

Many leaders were trained in environments where emotion was treated as unprofessional, where composure meant distance, and where credibility was associated with detachment. But in modern leadership, detachment reads as indifference. Authority without humanity no longer lands the way it once did.

This does not mean leaders should collapse emotionally in public. It means they must learn emotional containment.

The Discipline of Emotional Containment

Acknowledgment is not emotional collapse. It is emotional containment.

It requires leaders to name what people feel without becoming defensive, avoid minimizing language, resist the urge to fix emotion immediately, and stay present without being overtaken.

This is hard work. High-performing leaders are trained to act, not to sit with discomfort. But leadership communication demands restraint before resolution.

Containment also requires leaders to tolerate emotion without punishing it. When people are angry, leaders often want to correct them. When people are afraid, leaders often want to dismiss them. When people are grieving, leaders often want to hurry them.

Acknowledgment says: you are allowed to feel this.

That is not weakness. That is leadership.

A Public Leadership Scenario

When Residents Are Afraid and the Institution Sounds Procedural

In public service, the consequences of skipping acknowledgment are even greater. Images travel faster than context. Headlines move faster than explanations. Public trust is fragile and cumulative.

When a public safety incident occurs, or a service disruption impacts residents, leaders often default to procedure. "We are investigating." "We are reviewing." "We are following protocol."

Those statements may be true. They may even be necessary. But when they arrive without acknowledgment, the public hears something else. They hear indifference, evasion, and distance.

In moments where residents are afraid, procedural language alone feels like abandonment.

Acknowledgment sounds different. "We know people are scared." "We know families are asking whether they are safe." "We understand the frustration and fear this has created." "We want to begin by saying we see you, and this matters."

Then, and only then, do facts become useful. Because now you are speaking into a room that feels recognized, not brushed aside.

Political Leadership: The Cost of Sounding Scripted

Candidates and elected officials face a specific vulnerability. Every statement is interpreted as strategy. That makes leaders hesitant to acknowledge emotion, because emotion is often framed as weakness.

But the public does not punish emotion. The public punishes insincerity.

In political leadership, failure to acknowledge often sounds like this: "I understand people have concerns." "This is a distraction." "My record speaks for itself."

These are not acknowledgments. They are shields.

A real acknowledgment sounds like this: "I understand why people are upset." "I understand why this raised questions." "I want to speak first to the impact before I speak to the details."

That is not surrender. That is presence. And presence is what earns credibility when motives are questioned.

The Acknowledgment Ladder

How to Name Emotion Without Getting Stuck There

Some leaders fear acknowledgment because they do not know how to move from emotion to action.

They worry that once they open the door, they will not be able to close it.

This is where leaders need structure.

Use this sequence:

Step 1: Name it
"I know this is painful."
"I know people are angry."
"I know many are afraid."

Step 2: Legitimize the humanity, not every claim
"It makes sense that this would feel that way."
"I understand why this would create fear and frustration."

Step 3: Anchor your presence
"We are here."
"We are paying attention."
"We are taking this seriously."

Step 4: Transition to what comes next
"Here is what we know right now."
"Here is what we are still working to confirm."
"Here is when you will hear from us again."

Acknowledgment is not the end of the message.

It is the doorway that makes the message possible.

Phrases Leaders Should Stop Using

If you want to protect authority, remove the phrases that quietly insult the audience.

Replace these:

- "I know this is upsetting, but…"
- "With all due respect…"
- "Let me be clear" (when what follows is defensive)
- "At the end of the day…"
- "We apologize if anyone was offended"
- "This is being taken out of context"

With these:

- "I understand why this is upsetting."
- "I want to acknowledge the impact before I explain the details."
- "Here is what we know, and here is what we do not know yet."
- "Here is what we are doing next, and here is when you will hear from us again."

Authority is not protected by distance.

It is protected by alignment.

Why This Step Comes Second in C.A.L.M.

Centering yourself comes first because you cannot acknowledge others if you are unregulated yourself. Acknowledgment comes second because without it, nothing else works.

You cannot lead with facts if people feel unseen. You cannot model accountability if people feel dismissed. You cannot own the narrative if the emotional ground is unstable.

Acknowledgment prepares the room. It turns noise into receptivity, panic into possibility, and anger into a conversation instead of a combustion.

The Bridge Forward

Once emotion has been acknowledged, something shifts. Breathing slows. Defensiveness softens. People become capable of hearing difficult truths. Only then does clarity become possible.

In the next chapter, we move to the next discipline of calm leadership: leading with facts without weaponizing them. Because facts are powerful, but only when they are introduced into a space that is emotionally ready to receive them.

Acknowledgment does not end the work. It makes the work possible. And when leaders understand that, their voices stop escalating moments and start stabilizing them.

That is what calm leadership sounds like when the world is watching.

Chapter 5
Leading With Facts, Not Fear

How clarity stabilizes people when information is incomplete

**"Facts don't calm people by themselves.
They calm people when leaders use them with discipline."**
— On the Record

The Moment After Acknowledgment

Chapter 4 was about naming what people feel before asking them to hear anything else. This chapter begins where that step ends.

Acknowledgment earns attention. Clarity earns trust.

Once emotion has been named, people start reaching for footing. They want something solid. They want to know what is real, what is rumor, what is changing, and what is not. And this is where many leaders collapse the moment, not because they are cruel or careless, but because they are afraid.

They are afraid of the headline, of being wrong, of litigation, of backlash, and of what happens when the public learns what the leader has not fully figured out yet. Fear makes leaders treat facts like liabilities. But facts, delivered with discipline, are not liabilities. They are anchors.

When the Story Breaks Before the Message

By the time this particular tech industry CEO called me, the damage was already underway. The memo had leaked, not the final version, not the approved language, not the explanation leadership had debated and softened. Just enough. Enough to confirm what people feared most, spark speculation, and invite the press into a conversation employees had not yet been invited into themselves.

Slack channels were buzzing. Screenshots circulated. Group chats filled with half-questions and worst-case assumptions. A reporter emailed for comment before the executive team had finished debating whether to move the all-hands meeting up by an hour or delay it another day. The workforce was fully remote, scattered across time zones, watching fear move faster than facts.

This is the moment when most leaders panic. They panic because the narrative is moving without them, the facts are still forming, and silence now feels suspicious. And panic, once it enters leadership communication, makes leaders dangerous.

My job in that moment was not to help the CEO get ahead of the story. It was to slow it down.

Fear Is a Terrible Editor

The CEO's voice was tight when he asked the question leaders always ask when they feel exposed. "What should I say right now?"

I did not answer immediately. Instead, I asked him something that felt almost cruel in the moment. "What do you know for certain, and what are you still deciding?"

There was a long pause.

This is the discipline most leaders resist. When fear is loud, the instinct is to fill the space, to say something, anything, that restores a sense of control. But control is not what people are looking for in a crisis. They are looking for stability.

Stability does not come from speed. It comes from truth that can withstand revision.

Fear edits language poorly. It pushes leaders toward euphemisms instead of facts, reassurance instead of reality, and performance instead of presence. When leaders speak from fear, their words become brittle. They crack the moment new information emerges. And once credibility cracks, it rarely recovers fully.

Leading with facts is not about being cold. It is about being careful.

Facts Are Not Neutral

One of the most common mistakes leaders make is believing facts speak for themselves. They do not.

Facts are interpreted through emotion, history, and trust. Without leadership framing, facts can inflame fear just as easily as they can calm it. Facts do not erase pain. They do not soften loss. They do not make difficult decisions humane.

What facts do is limit imagination.

Fear thrives in ambiguity. When leaders avoid facts, people fill the gaps themselves with worst-case scenarios, whispered theories, and catastrophic assumptions. Facts constrain that spiral. They give people something solid to stand on, even when the ground is shifting.

This is why facts must be treated as anchors, not weapons. Anchors hold meaning in place. Weapons escalate conflict.

Leaders who use facts defensively often sound evasive. Leaders who avoid facts entirely sound deceptive. Leaders who use facts with discipline create stability even when certainty is gone.

The Difference Between Clarity and Reassurance

Many leaders confuse reassurance with leadership. They believe calming language is the same as stabilizing language. It is not.

Reassurance tries to remove anxiety. Clarity helps people survive anxiety.

Reassurance sounds like this: "Everything is under control." "There is nothing to worry about." "This will blow over." "We have it handled."

Clarity sounds like this: "Here is what we know right now." "Here is what we do not know yet." "Here is what we are doing next." "Here is when you will hear from us again."

Reassurance is fragile. Clarity is durable.

When the next fact arrives, reassurance collapses. Clarity adapts.

The Myth of "Total Transparency"

There is a dangerous myth in modern leadership culture that transparency means telling people everything you know the moment you know it.

That is not transparency.

That is emotional dumping disguised as honesty.

True transparency is structured. It is intentional. It respects the audience enough not to flood them with half-formed conclusions, internal debate, or speculative reassurance.

Before we drafted a single sentence for the all-hands meeting, we did three things:

1. **Separated facts from fears**
2. **Identified what could be said now without revision later**
3. **Built a communication cadence instead of a single announcement**

This is where many leaders fail.

They believe the all-hands meeting is the crisis. They treat it like a performance. One speech. One moment. One opportunity to "get it right."

But crises do not resolve in a single meeting.

They unfold.

Credibility is built in the unfolding, not the announcement.

The Four Types of Facts Leaders Must Manage

To lead with facts, leaders have to stop thinking of information as one category.

In crisis, facts come in layers.

1. Confirmed facts
What you know is true and can say without backtracking.

2. Operational facts
What is happening next, who is doing what, and what the process will look like.

3. Unconfirmed information
What you are still investigating and cannot responsibly state as true.

4. Emotional facts
What people are experiencing as true, even if it is not technically accurate.

Leaders often ignore emotional facts.

But emotional facts drive behavior.

If employees believe more layoffs are coming, productivity collapses.

If residents believe their water is unsafe, they will act on that belief long before a press release corrects it.

If the public believes leaders are hiding information, every future statement is received as spin.

Leading with facts means addressing all four categories with discipline.

Not all at once.

But intentionally.

Coaching the CEO Before the Cameras Turn On

The night before the all-hands meeting, we rehearsed privately. No slides. No script. Just voice, pacing, and restraint.

The CEO kept wanting to add more context, more justification, more explanation of how hard the decision had been. I stopped him.

"This is not about convincing people you struggled," I said. "It is about convincing them you are telling the truth."

There are phrases leaders reach for instinctively during layoffs that almost always backfire: "This was an incredibly difficult decision for us." "We are all in this together." "We are like a family."

These phrases center leadership emotion instead of employee reality. In moments of loss, people do not want to know how hard it was for you to decide. They want to know whether you respect them enough to be honest.

So we removed every sentence that tried to manage feelings instead of facts. The tone shifted. Not colder or warmer. Clearer.

Leading Humans Through a Screen

Remote crises introduce a level of distance leaders consistently underestimate. You cannot read the room the same way. You cannot feel the emotional temperature. You cannot see who is dissociating, shutting down, or spiraling quietly off-camera.

So leaders compensate with words. They rush. They over-script. They talk through the hardest moments because silence feels unbearable.

I told the CEO something that felt counterintuitive. "Slow down. Let the silence work."

Silence, when intentional, gives people space to absorb facts without panic. It communicates steadiness. It signals that you are not afraid of the truth landing.

Humane leadership does not require warmth. It requires steadiness.

When the Press Knows Before Your People

Because of the leak, the CEO had to address what leaders dread most: employees learning about their own job loss from the media.

There is no perfect response to that. But there is a credible one.

He said it plainly. "You should have heard this from us first. That did not happen. And I am sorry."

No deflection. No legal language. No blame.

Facts land differently when leaders stop pretending they control everything. That single sentence repaired a small piece of the relationship before the hardest details arrived.

The Discipline of "What We Know, What We Don't, What's Next"

When leaders do not have complete information, they often do one of two things. They speculate, or they freeze. Both are credibility killers.

Discipline looks like this: here is what we know. Here is what we do not know yet. Here is what we are doing to find out. Here is when you will hear from us next.

That cadence does not require certainty. It requires integrity. It is also the fastest way to stop rumor from becoming policy in people's minds, because most rumor is not about curiosity. It is about fear trying to protect itself.

Facts Without Cadence Still Create Panic

Many leaders believe that if they deliver one clear message, the crisis will settle. It will not.

People do not calm down because you spoke once. They stabilize when they trust the rhythm of your presence.

That is why we established one non-negotiable rule: no day without communication.

Even if the update was small. Even if nothing had changed. Even if the answer was still, "We do not know yet."

Predictability became the antidote to fear. People do not need perfection. They need rhythm. And rhythm allows people to plan, breathe, and reorient.

The Day After Is Where Trust Is Decided

Most leaders believe surviving the announcement means the crisis is over. It is not.

The next day, remaining employees log in afraid. Productivity collapses. Survivor guilt surfaces. Rumors continue. Trust hangs by a thread.

This is where facts stop being a message and become a practice.

Facts must live in what leaders do next:

- Are leaders available for questions, or do they disappear?
- Do updates arrive consistently, or only when pressured?
- Are leaders clear about what changed, or vague to avoid discomfort?

- Do leaders correct misinformation quickly, or let it spread because it is inconvenient?

Every one of those decisions is communication.

Every one.

When Facts Become Weapons

Facts can stabilize, or they can be used to punish.

Some leaders weaponize facts to win arguments. They use numbers to dismiss pain. They use policy to erase impact. They use technical truth to avoid moral truth.

This is how leaders end up saying things like: "Technically, we followed protocol." "According to the data, this is not significant." "We are in compliance." "Legally, we are covered."

Those sentences may be true. But they are not leadership. They are shields.

Facts should be used to reduce panic, not to reduce accountability. The moment facts become a defense against humanity, they stop calming anyone. They start inflaming everyone.

Failure Case Study

When Facts Are Delayed and Fear Takes Over

Not all leaders choose this discipline.

In the early days of the Boeing 737 MAX crisis, facts were available. They were incomplete, but they were sufficient to warrant caution. Instead, leadership communication minimized risk. Internal discussions emphasized technical compliance rather than human consequence. Public statements reassured safety while questions mounted.

Families and the flying public were left with the sense that reassurance was being prioritized over truth.

What began as a crisis of engineering became a crisis of credibility. Each delayed acknowledgment, each defensive clarification, and each narrowly framed statement amplified suspicion.

The lesson is stark. When leaders delay facts to protect reputation, they sacrifice trust. Fear does not recede when leaders withhold information. It multiplies.

Success Case Study

Johnson & Johnson and the Discipline of Truth

In moments of crisis, facts rarely arrive neatly packaged. They arrive fractured, incomplete, and frightening.

The Tylenol crisis of 1982 remains one of the clearest examples of what it looks like to lead with facts rather than fear. Seven people died after taking cyanide-laced Tylenol capsules. Johnson & Johnson did not know who was responsible or whether more products were contaminated.

What leadership did know was this: people were dying.

Instead of waiting for certainty, every decision was anchored to one principle. Public safety came first. The company recalled 31 million bottles nationwide. Leaders spoke plainly about what they knew and what they did not. They corrected misinformation quickly and refused to speculate.

They did not promise certainty. They promised responsibility.

And trust followed.

When leaders communicate with that level of discipline, facts stop sounding cold. They start sounding credible.

The Truth About "Saying Too Much"

Leaders often fear that facts will make things worse. They worry that telling the truth will spark panic.

Sometimes truth is frightening. But panic usually comes from something else.

Panic comes from unpredictability. It comes from silence. It comes from contradiction. It comes from "we will get back to you" with no timeline. It comes from leaders who speak confidently today and revise tomorrow without acknowledgment.

People can endure hard facts. What they cannot endure is the sense that the ground is shifting beneath them while leadership pretends it is not.

What This Chapter Is Really About

This chapter is not about layoffs. Layoffs are simply the crucible.

This chapter is about the moment when fear pressures you to speak beyond what you know, when silence tempts you to wait too long, and when optics threaten to override ethics.

Leading with facts is a refusal. A refusal to dramatize. A refusal to speculate. A refusal to soothe yourself at the expense of others.

It is choosing steadiness when fear is loud. It is understanding that credibility is not built by knowing everything. It is built by telling the truth you can stand behind and returning with updates you can sustain.

The Leaders People Remember Are the Clearest Ones

Years from now, people will not remember every sentence you said. They will remember whether you lied, whether you hid, whether you respected them enough to tell the truth, and whether you showed up again the next day.

Facts do not make leaders cold. Fear does.

Facts, delivered with discipline, are how leaders protect dignity when certainty is gone.

What's Next

Chapter 5 answers the question: what do I say when I do not have all the answers?

Chapter 6 answers the harder one: what do I do when I get it wrong?

Because facts alone do not rebuild trust. Accountability does. And accountability, modeled in public, determines whether leadership survives the moment or is defined by it.

Chapter 6:
Modeling Accountability When Everyone Is Watching

How leaders retain trust after failure, missteps, and harm

"Accountability is not what you say when something goes wrong. It is what you are willing to carry when it would be easier to put it down."
— On the Record

Accountability Is Where Leadership Gets Real

Accountability is the moment leadership stops performing and starts standing still long enough to be seen.

Most leaders believe accountability begins when something goes wrong. In reality, it begins earlier, at the moment a leader decides whether they will remain visible when the narrative turns uncomfortable. Anyone can speak when decisions are applauded. Far fewer are willing to speak when the cost becomes public. That is the real test.

Accountability is not an apology tour. It is not a carefully worded statement issued after legal approval. It is not a temporary appearance followed by strategic disappearance. Accountability is the decision to stay present when retreat would be easier.

When accountability is modeled well, trust bends without breaking. People may disagree with the outcome. They may challenge the judgment. They may even feel disappointed or hurt. But they do not feel deceived. They do not feel erased.

When accountability is avoided, trust fractures quietly, often long before leaders realize it is gone. There is rarely an immediate collapse. Instead, there is erosion. Fewer questions are asked in meetings. Candor disappears from teams. Side conversations multiply. Skepticism grows. People comply, but they stop believing.

I have spent my career watching the difference.

I have watched leaders step forward and absorb the weight of their decisions, naming harm plainly, answering hard questions without flinching, and remaining visible long after the moment stopped trending. I have also watched leaders vanish behind silence, letting lawyers, human resources departments, or middle managers absorb the impact of choices they themselves made.

The distinction between those two paths determines whether a crisis becomes a chapter of credibility or the beginning of decline.

This chapter is about that distinction. Not in theory, but in practice. When the cameras are on. When the pressure is high. When the truth cannot be delegated.

What Real Accountability Actually Sounds Like

Most leaders think accountability starts with the words "I'm sorry." It does not.

True accountability starts with "I own this."

Apologies are emotional. Responsibility is structural. One acknowledges feeling. The other commits to consequence and change. People can sense the difference immediately.

A leader can apologize without ever taking responsibility. A leader cannot take responsibility without changing posture.

Real accountability includes four elements. The absence of any one of them weakens the whole.

Clarity about what happened

This means naming the moment honestly, without jargon or euphemism. Not "a misalignment occurred," but "we made a decision that caused harm." Clarity respects the intelligence of the people affected.

Ownership without deflection

Ownership means resisting the urge to explain yourself out of accountability. It means not hiding behind committees, market conditions, or vague references to "the organization." Leadership requires singular responsibility, even when decisions were collective.

Impact acknowledgment without minimization

Impact is not defined by intent. It is defined by experience. Leaders lose credibility the moment they argue with how people feel harmed. Accountability means recognizing impact even when it was not anticipated.

Corrective action without performance

This is the hardest part. It requires doing the work when no one is watching. Changing systems. Reallocating resources. Altering behavior. Not announcing accountability, but practicing it.

Anything less may sound polite, but it will not rebuild trust.

I often tell leaders this: if your accountability statement could be issued by any organization in any crisis, it is not accountable enough. Accountability is personal. It has fingerprints. It sounds like someone standing in front of their decisions instead of hiding behind process.

When Accountability Is Avoided: The Corporate Retreat

In the years following 2020, corporate America made some of the loudest moral declarations in modern history.

Companies issued statements affirming racial justice. They pledged billions toward equity initiatives. They created new executive roles, launched task forces, and promised that diversity, equity, and inclusion were not trends, but transformations.

Employees believed them.
Communities believed them.
Many leaders believed them too.

And then, quietly, many of those promises disappeared.

Budgets were "realigned."
Teams were "streamlined."
Priorities were "refocused."

What struck me was not just the reversal.
It was the silence.

There were no all-hands conversations explaining the shift. No acknowledgment that commitments once framed as moral imperatives were now being reconsidered. No ownership of the decision to pull back.

Departments were dismantled without explanation. Leaders who had once been vocal advocates stopped mentioning the work entirely. Accountability was replaced by euphemism.

This was not neutrality.
It was abdication.

Silence communicated what leaders would not say aloud. The commitments were conditional. The values were subject to pressure. Courage had an expiration date.

Employees noticed immediately. Customers noticed. Partners noticed. Communities noticed.

The message was not simply that priorities had changed. The message was that promises could be revoked without explanation.

I watched leaders struggle to understand why trust evaporated so quickly, why morale collapsed, and why credibility eroded even among those who once believed deeply in the mission.

The answer was simple.

They changed direction without changing posture.

If leaders had said, "We are making a different decision, and here is why," the reaction may still have been painful. But it would have been honest. Honesty allows people to grieve, disagree, and adapt.

Silence does not soften impact.
It multiplies it.

When leaders will not explain their choices, people assume the explanation is worse than the truth.

A Personal Reckoning With Responsibility

I know this moment intimately, not just as an observer, but as a participant.

When I stepped into a Chief Diversity Officer role in the technology sector, it felt like the culmination of everything I had worked toward. I was no longer advising from the outside. I was embedded in strategy, implementation, and results.

This was different from consulting. As a consultant, you influence from proximity. As a C-suite leader, you own outcomes.

I built teams.
I shaped culture.
I stood in front of employees, partners, policymakers, and external audiences and said, "This organization means what it says."

I believed it.

Then leadership changed.

What followed was not dramatic. There were no fiery memos or public confrontations. It was quieter and far more damaging.

Budgets were reduced without explanation.
Teams were cut incrementally, then dramatically.
Initiatives once championed were paused, then erased.

There was no statement that said, "We are stepping back from this commitment."
There was no acknowledgment of the shift.
There was no ownership of the reversal.

There was only silence.

For the first time in my career, I was on the other side of accountability failure.

Employees came to me with questions I could no longer answer. Partners asked for reassurance I could no longer provide. Communities who had trusted our word felt misled.

Those of us who had been visible stewards of the message were left holding credibility leadership no longer protected.

That is what accountability failure looks like from the inside.

It does not just erode trust externally.
It fractures it internally.
It places moral weight on the wrong shoulders.

And it changes you.

When leaders refuse to model accountability, they leave their people exposed.

When Accountability Is Modeled Well: Visibility With Consequence

Contrast that with leaders who understand that accountability must be visible and costly to be credible.

In 2018, Starbucks faced national outrage after two Black men were arrested in a Philadelphia store for waiting for a friend. The video went viral within hours.

What happened next mattered more than the incident itself.

The chief executive officer did not hide behind statements. He flew to Philadelphia. He met the men face to face. He acknowledged harm without defensiveness.

Then he made a decision that cost the company millions by closing more than 8,000 stores nationwide for racial bias training.

Was it perfect? No.
Was it criticized? Absolutely.

But it was accountable.

Starbucks did not pretend the incident was isolated. Leadership accepted responsibility for the environment they had created and took visible action.

Accountability is not about being flawless.
It is about being unmistakably present.

People may debate effectiveness.
Few questioned seriousness.

That distinction preserved trust even amid disagreement.

Accountability Is a Posture, Not a Moment

One of the most common mistakes leaders make is treating accountability as a single event. A statement. A meeting. A press conference.

Accountability is not an appearance. It is a posture.

I have coached leaders through layoffs, restructurings, and public backlash where the hardest part was not the announcement. It was the day after. The unanswered emails.

The teams still showing up uncertain. The managers trying to stabilize morale.

The leaders who regained trust were not the ones who sounded perfect on day one. They were the ones who stayed visible on day ten.

Consistency is accountability's proof.

Why Accountability Is Harder at the Top

Accountability becomes more difficult as power increases. Senior leaders face pressures that do not exist at lower levels. Legal risk is higher. Media scrutiny is relentless. Board expectations conflict with public perception. Every word carries permanence.

This environment teaches leaders to prioritize protection. But protection and accountability are not the same thing.

Accountability requires leaders to tolerate discomfort without rushing to control it. It requires acknowledging harm without knowing how it will be received. It requires staying present while criticism unfolds publicly.

Many leaders equate authority with certainty. Accountability challenges that belief. It asks leaders to demonstrate strength through honesty rather than confidence.

The leaders who manage this well understand something critical. Authority is not diminished by accountability. It is strengthened by it.

People do not lose respect for leaders who own their decisions. They lose respect for leaders who hide behind process or disappear when trust is tested.

Accountability signals courage. And courage is credibility at scale.

Five Ways Leaders Accidentally Avoid Accountability

Most accountability failures are not intentional. They are behavioral. Leaders believe they are being responsible when they are actually retreating. The patterns repeat across industries and institutions.

The first is delegation disguised as leadership. Leaders hand accountability to legal teams, communications staff, or middle managers and call it process. The public hears avoidance.

The second is technical truth replacing moral truth. Leaders rely on policy language, compliance statements, and procedural explanations that may be accurate but feel dismissive of harm.

The third is overcorrection through silence. Leaders fear saying the wrong thing, so they say nothing. Silence is interpreted as indifference or guilt.

The fourth is one-and-done communication. Leaders issue a single statement and move on, assuming the moment has passed. Trust does not work on press release timelines.

The fifth is defensiveness disguised as clarification. Leaders frame accountability as correcting misunderstanding instead of acknowledging impact. This shifts focus away from responsibility and toward self-protection.

None of these behaviors feel unethical in the moment. They feel cautious. They feel smart. They feel safe.

But they erode trust precisely because they center the leader instead of the people affected.

Accountability requires leaders to resist instinct and choose exposure.

What Accountability Looks Like the Day After

Most leaders believe accountability ends when the statement is issued. It does not.

The real test begins the next morning.

The day after a crisis announcement is when trust is either quietly rebuilt or quietly abandoned. This is when employees decide whether leadership meant what it said. This is when external audiences determine whether accountability was performative or real.

Accountability after the statement looks like presence, not polish. It looks like leaders remaining visible even when there is no new information to share. It looks like answering the same question more than once without irritation. It looks like correcting the record when facts change instead of pretending they did not.

In organizations where accountability holds, leaders do four things consistently in the days and weeks that follow.

They stay accessible. Leaders make themselves available to employees, partners, and stakeholders instead of retreating behind layers of communication staff. They do not outsource discomfort.

They communicate on a predictable cadence. Even when nothing has changed, leaders say so. Silence creates suspicion. Consistency creates stability.

They acknowledge when information evolves. When facts change, accountable leaders name the change and explain why. They do not quietly revise their position and hope no one notices.

They connect words to action. Accountability is reinforced when people can see how leadership decisions align with what was promised. Process changes. Resource shifts. Policy updates. Follow-through makes accountability visible.

Leaders who disappear after the announcement teach people that accountability was temporary. Leaders who remain present teach people that accountability is a value, not a tactic.

This distinction is where trust lives.

The Line Accountability Draws

Every leader crosses a line at some point.

On one side is image management. On the other is stewardship.

Image asks, "How do I look?"
Stewardship asks, "What do I owe?"

Accountability lives firmly on the second side of that line. Once you cross it, leadership changes.

The Bridge Forward

Accountability answers the question:
Will you stand with what you said?

Narrative answers a different one:
Will you define what it means?

Too many leaders believe accepting responsibility is enough.

It is not.

If you do not define the meaning of the moment, someone else will.

They will not do it with your values, your context, or your long-term credibility in mind.

That is where we go next.

PART III: OWNING THE NARRATIVE

Chapter 7
Owning the Story Before It Owns You

Why proactive communication protects leadership

"If not now, then when?" — Roxie

The Story Vacuum

A crisis begins the moment you lose control of meaning. Not because you stopped caring or suddenly became incompetent, but because you underestimated how quickly meaning forms when people feel confused, afraid, or betrayed.

In the space between what happened and what has been explained, people do what humans have always done in uncertainty. They create meaning. They fill gaps. They connect dots that were never meant to touch. They search for a villain, a motive, and a reason to feel safe again.

This is not irrational. It is survival.

And story control is not ego. It is stewardship.

When leaders hesitate, speak vaguely, or go silent, they do not pause the narrative. They abandon it. Silence creates a vacuum, and vacuums never remain empty for long. They fill with rumor, screenshots, speculation, and commentary. They fill with the loudest voice in the room, not the most accurate one. And once a story hardens in the public mind, facts have to work twice as hard just to be heard.

This is why narrative control is not a branding exercise. It is a leadership responsibility.

Owning the story before it owns you means you do not wait for a headline to introduce you. You do not wait for a leak to define you. You do not wait for backlash to tell you what your values were supposed to be. You practice being the narrator of your own leadership.

Because leadership, at its core, is public meaning-making.

People are not only watching how you respond. They are watching how you interpret what happened. They are listening for whether you understand the impact. They are tracking whether your behavior aligns with your values. And they are deciding, in real time, whether you are safe to trust.

This chapter is about the discipline of proactive communication. How to frame moments before crisis forces explanation. How to prevent silence from becoming surrender. How to build narrative consistency that protects your leadership long after the moment passes.

Roxie and the Lesson of Speaking Before the Rumor Becomes Law

My grandmother Roxie did not have a communications team. She did not use phrases like narrative strategy or reputation management. But she understood something many modern leaders do not.

The first version of the story often becomes the only version people remember.

In a small Mississippi town, news traveled fast and rarely traveled clean. A raised eyebrow could become a confession. A half-heard conversation could turn into scandal. And if you did not address something directly, you might find yourself defending a story you never told.

Roxie practiced what I now recognize as proactive clarity. If someone misunderstood her, she corrected it early. If something felt off in the community, she asked questions directly. If conflict was brewing, she did not stay out of it until it exploded. She showed up before the fire reached the curtains.

I watched her walk straight into spaces where confusion lived and speak plainly, without drama or defensiveness. Not because she wanted attention, but because she understood that silence does not keep the peace. Silence keeps the confusion.

She used to tell me, "Baby, folks will believe what they can repeat."

That line followed me into every boardroom I have ever entered.

People do not only want the truth. They want a story they can carry, explain, and repeat. If you do not give them one, they will borrow one from whoever is willing to speak first.

Roxie also believed deeply in timing. "If not now, then when?" was not a motivational quote. It was a warning. She meant that if you wait until the story hardens, you will spend twice as long trying to soften it. If you wait until people are angry, everything you say will sound defensive. If you wait until the cameras arrive, you will start performing instead of leading.

Leaders who shape the story speak early enough to stabilize meaning, and they keep speaking long enough to sustain trust.

Narrative Control as Stewardship

Some people hear "own the narrative" and think it means spinning facts, managing optics, or winning perception battles.

That is not what this is.

Owning the narrative is stewardship. It is the responsibility to define a moment accurately, ethically, and humanely before misinformation defines it for you.

At its simplest, narrative stewardship answers four questions clearly and consistently:

1. **What happened**
2. **What it means**
3. **What we are doing**
4. **What people should expect next**

When leaders provide that frame, they do not eliminate disagreement, but they prevent confusion from turning into fear.

When leaders refuse to provide that frame, people interpret events alone. And when people interpret events alone, they interpret them through fear.

This is why narrative ownership is not self promotion. It is public service. It is leadership made visible.

Chapter 6 was about accountability, what to do when you have failed, harmed, or misstepped. Chapter 7 is about something that often comes earlier.

How to prevent a moment from becoming a collapse by owning the story before it becomes your identity.

The Three Clocks

In every high pressure moment, three clocks start running at the same time.

The operational clock measures what is actually happening in real time: the facts, the decisions, the logistics.

The emotional clock measures what people feel and what they fear: uncertainty, anger, grief, betrayal.

The narrative clock measures what people believe is happening: the story forming in group chats, headlines, Slack channels, and social feeds.

Most leaders fixate on the operational clock. They focus on solving the problem. That matters. But when leaders ignore the emotional and narrative clocks, the problem multiplies.

People do not only respond to what happened. They respond to what they think happened, what they think you knew, and what they think you tried to hide.

This is where leaders get trapped.

They say, "We did not have all the facts yet," and that may be true operationally. But narratively, the story has already formed.

The goal is not perfection. The goal is direction.

What Silence Communicates

Silence is never neutral. It is interpreted.

When leaders go quiet, people do not assume diligence. They assume avoidance. Silence often sounds like this: we do not care. We hope you forget. We are waiting for lawyers. We are afraid of accountability. We do not respect you enough to explain. Even when none of those things are true.

This is why silence becomes surrender. Not because you lacked a statement, but because you surrendered meaning.

In moments of uncertainty, people trust the leader who helps them make meaning, not the leader who hides until it feels safe to speak.

The First Frame Wins

One of the hardest truths in crisis leadership is this: the first credible frame usually wins. Not forever, and not in every case, but long enough to set a tone that is difficult to undo.

This is why leaders must stop thinking in terms of responding and start thinking in terms of framing. A response answers a question. A frame tells people what to do with the answer.

If you do not frame your moment, someone else will. And they will not frame it with your values.

A Signature Moment

The Leaked Memo Before the Layoff

Layoffs expose narrative weakness quickly. Not because they are always avoidable, but because they demand moral clarity. People are not only asking what happened. They are asking, who are we to you.

I have helped leaders prepare for large layoffs, including moments when teams were fully remote, exhausted by the pandemic, and scanning every calendar invite for signs of bad news. In one situation, we came dangerously close to losing the story before leadership ever spoke.

We had planned a company-wide all-hands announcement. The intent was humane. The structure was thoughtful. Then a memo leaked, not only internally, but externally. Employees saw screenshots first. Reporters reached out before the CEO had spoken.

Now there were two crises: a workforce crisis and a narrative crisis.

The meaning people attached to the leak formed immediately. They were going to do this without telling us. They were already talking to the press. They decided we do not matter.

This is where leaders often retreat. They pause. They tighten language. They delay.

Delay, in that moment, would have felt like abandonment.

So we owned the story immediately. We moved up the CEO's message. We acknowledged the leak directly. We spoke to employees before the media. We told the truth simply.

The CEO opened with clarity, not theater: "I want you to hear this from me, directly. Some information is circulating that should not have been. I will not ask you to ignore it. I will tell you the truth."

That choice stabilized meaning. Not because the news was good, but because people felt respected.

We provided a clear frame of what was known, what was changing, what support looked like, and what would happen next. Then we prepared for the day after, when trust is truly decided.

Narrative ownership was not a statement. It was a sustained posture.

Explanation Versus Ownership

Many leaders believe they are communicating when they are actually explaining. Explanation happens after the story has already formed. Ownership happens before it hardens.

Explanation sounds like this: let me clarify. That is not what happened. You misunderstood.

Ownership sounds like this: here is what happened. Here is what it means. Here is what we are doing. Here is what comes next.

Clarifying is not wrong. But if clarification becomes your strategy, you are always behind.

The Leadership Frame

Here is a simple way to test whether you are leading the story or chasing it.

If your communication begins with what you want people to stop believing, you are already late. If your communication begins with what you want people to understand, you are still leading.

Owning the story means you communicate forward, not backward.

A Mirror Before the Method

Before we go deeper, it helps to recognize familiar traps. Many leaders see themselves here:

- **Delay disguised as diligence**
- **Legal language replacing leadership language**
- **Explaining instead of naming**
- **One statement with no follow through**
- **Waiting for certainty instead of providing direction**

If any of these feel familiar, this chapter is for you.

Case Study: When the Story Owns You

United Airlines

The United Airlines passenger removal incident became a global lesson in narrative failure.

A video circulated showing a passenger being violently dragged from an overbooked flight. The public reaction was immediate and visceral. People did not see a policy issue. They saw humiliation.

United's initial response framed the incident procedurally. Early statements emphasized policy adherence and described the passenger in language that felt cold and detached from what people had just witnessed.

The result was not just outrage, but narrative collapse.

The public story became clear: this company values process over people.

By the time leadership shifted tone and issued a more human apology, the narrative had already hardened. The damage was not caused solely by the incident, but by the failure to acknowledge meaning quickly enough.

When leaders miss the first window to interpret what people experienced, they rarely get another one.

Case Study: When You Own the Story

Domino's Pizza

Domino's provides a powerful contrast.

Facing widespread criticism about product quality, the company did not deny perception or hide behind marketing. Instead, they acknowledged the criticism openly. They admitted what was not working. Then they invited the public into the process of change.

Their campaign showed chefs reading negative reviews aloud. They documented recipe changes. They made the public a witness to improvement.

This was narrative ownership with integrity. Domino's did not try to argue people into liking them. They showed transformation in real time.

The story shifted because the company owned it.

The Five Principles of Narrative Ownership

Leaders who build narrative resilience practice five disciplines consistently.

1. Name the moment early, before it names you
Do not wait for the headline to become your introduction.

2. Speak in a stable cadence

Even when information is incomplete, presence must be consistent.

3. Frame with values, not defensiveness

Values clarify meaning. Defensiveness signals fear.

4. Repeat with consistency

Repetition is not redundancy. It is reassurance. People do not trust what they hear once. They trust what holds.

5. Build the day after narrative, not just the announcement

The story is decided in what you do next, not what you say first.

Narrative ownership is not a speech. It is a system.

The Narrative Bank

The leaders who perform best under pressure are rarely improvising. They have built a narrative bank in advance: a clear articulation of values, purpose, non negotiables, and accountability standards.

When pressure hits, they do not scramble for identity. They speak from it.

You do not become a different leader in crisis. You become a clearer version of who you already were.

This is why narrative work begins before the crisis.

What do you stand for.
What do you refuse to do.
What do you owe the people you lead.
What is your standard for accountability.

What is your standard for truth.
What is your standard for dignity.

When those answers are clear, your crisis communication becomes faster, not because you rush, but because you do not have to invent meaning.

When Silence Is Wisdom, and When It Is Harm

There are moments when silence is appropriate. An investigation is active. A family needs privacy. A threat requires operational containment. Facts are changing too quickly to speak responsibly.

But even in those moments, silence must be paired with visible commitment and clear timing.

We are aware. We are investigating. We will update you by this time. Here is what we can say now. Here is what we will not do, even while we investigate.

Silence only becomes surrender when you disappear and leave people alone with their fear.

From Ownership to Responsibility

Owning the story before it owns you is a personal leadership discipline. But leadership evolves.

Chapter 7 is about owning your story. Chapter 8 is about what happens when your story is no longer yours alone.

Because when you speak for institutions, for communities, and for people whose voices carry less power, narrative ownership becomes responsibility. Visibility becomes burden. And words must protect more than reputation.

They must protect dignity.

The next chapter is where leadership stops being personal and becomes representative. And that is where the weight truly shifts.

Chapter 8
Speaking for Institutions, Not Just Yourself

The burden and responsibility of representing others

"When you speak for an institution, your voice carries people who will never get the microphone."
— On the Record

When the Voice Becomes a Vessel

There is a moment in leadership when your voice stops belonging to you.

It does not arrive with a title change, a press release, or a corner office. It arrives quietly, often mid-sentence, when you realize what you are saying will not be heard as opinion. It will be received as position. Your words will be quoted as policy. Your tone will be interpreted as intent. Your silence will be treated as strategy.

This is the moment leadership becomes stewardship.

When you speak for an institution, you are no longer communicating only for yourself. You are carrying history, power, and consequence. You are shaping trust on behalf of people who may never sit in the room, never approve the language, and never have the chance to correct the record once your words are public.

Institutional speech is permanent in ways personal speech is not.

Screenshots last. Policies outlive people. Communities remember.

A single sentence, poorly framed or defensively delivered, can resurface years later as evidence that an institution knew, dismissed, or deprioritized the people it was meant to serve. Words spoken under pressure do not fade. They harden. They become precedent.

This is why institutional voice requires discipline. Not perfection. Not polish. Discipline.

Institutions are remembered less for what they say when things are calm and more for how they speak when people are afraid, angry, or hurting. In those moments, the public is not listening for fluency. They are listening for alignment.

The Long Arc of Speaking for Others

I did not step into institutional voice all at once. I grew into it in phases, each one increasing the weight of what my words carried.

Early in my career, I represented companies from the outside. I was the advisor, the strategist, the person helping shape language leaders would deliver. I understood responsibility, but it was indirect. My voice influenced outcomes, but it was not the final one. If the message landed poorly, it could be revised. If leadership chose a different path, the consequences belonged to them.

Mid-career, I became something different. I was no longer just advising leadership. I was leadership.

I represented companies to their employees. I spoke internally on behalf of decisions I did not always originate, but that I was responsible for explaining. I learned what it meant to translate strategy into meaning for people whose livelihoods were affected by it.

Then I crossed another threshold entirely.

I became a spokesperson.

I wrote statements that would be read on camera. I prepared leaders for stages where every word could be clipped, replayed, and reinterpreted. I stood in front of microphones knowing that what I said would not be heard as my perspective. It would be received as the institution's truth.

That shift changes you.

Because when you speak publicly for an organization, you are no longer managing messaging. You are managing consequence.

You learn quickly that cleverness is dangerous, that defensiveness travels faster than facts, and that people do not separate the speaker from the system.

And you learn this truth above all others:

When you speak for an institution, you inherit the moral weight of what it does and does not say.

The Dangerous Myth of Neutrality

One of the most persistent myths in institutional leadership is the belief that neutrality is possible.

It is not.

Institutions do not exist outside of context. They are shaped by history, power, and memory. Every organization carries a past, whether acknowledged or denied, and every statement is filtered through that past before it is received.

When leaders claim neutrality in moments that demand moral clarity, the public does not hear restraint.

They hear avoidance.

Silence, delay, or overly legal language is rarely interpreted as prudence. More often, it signals fear, indifference, or quiet alignment with harm.

Neutrality is not misunderstood. **It is experienced.**

Institutions often default to what feels safest inside the building. Language engineered to survive review. Language designed to offend no one. Language that delays acknowledgment until certainty feels absolute.

But harm does not wait for certainty.

And communities do not experience delay as strategy. They experience it as dismissal.

True institutional leadership requires interrupting the instinct to hide behind neutrality and choosing clarity even when it feels uncomfortable.

Because the public does not measure you by what you wanted to say.

They measure you by what your words did.

The People in the Sentence

One of the quiet truths of institutional leadership is that you are often speaking for people you will never meet. The frontline worker clocking in before dawn. The resident navigating bureaucracy in the middle of a crisis. The employee without the power or protection to speak publicly. The family waiting for answers with the television on, watching your statement crawl across the bottom of the screen.

Somewhere, someone is standing at a counter holding paperwork they do not understand, waiting for a decision your words helped shape. Somewhere else, a parent is deciding whether the institution responsible for their safety is worthy of trust.

When you speak, they are being judged through your voice.

That is why institutional communication cannot be driven by ego, applause, or cleverness. It must be driven by care, accuracy, and restraint.

Before any major statement, I learned to ask one grounding question: does this protect the people we serve, or does it protect us?

That single question changes the posture of the room. It forces leaders to confront whether their instinct is stewardship or self-preservation. It exposes the temptation every institution faces in a crisis: to protect the institution first.

The Institutional Nervous System

Leaders have nervous systems. So do institutions.

When pressure hits, institutions tighten. They become risk-averse. They become approval-heavy. They become language-phobic. Messages are pulled inward, into rooms with fewer people and more lawyers. Decisions slow down, not to be careful, but to be safe.

Not safe for the public. Safe from liability. Safe from headlines. Safe from blame.

You can feel the institutional nervous system in certain phrases: "We take this matter seriously." "We are reviewing the situation." "We are committed to our values." "We cannot comment at this time."

These phrases are not always wrong. But without specificity, they become placeholders for avoidance. The public knows the difference between an investigation and an evasion.

When an institution is dysregulated, it becomes obsessed with controlling language instead of stabilizing reality. Communication fails not because the facts are unclear, but because the posture is.

Representative Leadership Has Two Audiences

When you speak for an institution, you are always speaking to at least two audiences.

There is the internal audience: employees, staff, frontline teams, and stakeholders inside the building who need clarity, dignity, and direction.

There is the external audience: residents, customers, families, media, partners, regulators, and communities who need truth, accountability, and confidence.

Most institutions struggle to serve both. They protect internal operations and alienate the public. Or they perform for the public and betray their own people.

Stewardship is the skill of holding both.

Internal trust collapses when employees feel thrown under the bus. External trust collapses when the public feels lied to, minimized, or managed.

Institutional voice must do what individual voice rarely has to do:

Communicate with integrity in both directions at once.

Case Study: When Institutional Voice Fails (United Airlines)

In 2017, a video circulated showing a passenger being violently removed from a United Airlines flight after the airline overbooked the plane. The footage was graphic. The man was dragged down the aisle, bloodied, as other passengers screamed in shock.

The public reaction was immediate and visceral.

What followed turned a crisis into a case study in narrative failure.

United's initial response described the incident as a need to "re-accommodate" passengers. Internally, leadership circulated a memo defending employees and framing the situation as a policy issue rather than a human one.

This language mattered.

Because while the company focused on procedure, the public focused on harm.

The gap between experience and explanation widened with every statement. The tone sounded clinical where people expected compassion. The framing felt dismissive where people needed accountability.

By the time leadership shifted toward a more human apology, the narrative had hardened.

United had lost control of meaning not simply because the incident occurred, but because the institution failed to demonstrate that it understood what people had just witnessed.

This is the cost of institutional misalignment.

When leaders speak as if they are managing an inconvenience instead of acknowledging harm, trust collapses. The audience does not hear defense.

They hear detachment.

The lesson is simple and unforgiving:

When institutions fail to acknowledge emotion before explaining policy, they do not sound neutral. They sound inhumane.

Case Study: When Institutional Voice Holds (Ben & Jerry's)

If **United Airlines** illustrates failure, **Ben & Jerry's** illustrates something rarer: institutional voice exercised with intention, clarity, and consequence.

From its founding, Ben & Jerry's positioned itself as more than an ice cream company. Social justice, environmental responsibility, and political engagement were not seasonal marketing campaigns. They were embedded into the brand's identity.

This distinction matters. When an institution speaks consistently over time, its voice builds character.

In 2021, Ben & Jerry's announced it would stop selling its ice cream in Israeli settlements in the occupied Palestinian territories, stating that doing so was inconsistent with its values. The backlash was immediate and global. Political leaders condemned the decision. Some U.S. states invoked anti-BDS laws to divest from the company's parent organization, **Unilever**. Accusations flew. Media scrutiny intensified.

This was not a messaging error. It was a values decision with real consequence.

What makes this case instructive is not whether one agrees with the position. It is how the institution handled the weight of speaking for others.

Ben & Jerry's did not retreat into silence. They did not soften the language to appease critics. They clarified, contextualized, and reaffirmed their values.

They understood something many institutions avoid. When you speak for an institution, you are not just expressing belief. You are accepting consequence on behalf of everyone connected to you: employees, partners, customers, and stakeholders.

The tension between Ben & Jerry's and its parent company became public, exposing a rare clash between values-based speech and corporate risk management. Even then, Ben & Jerry's remained aligned with the identity it had spent decades establishing.

This is institutional stewardship. Not because it was painless. Not because it was universally liked. But because it was intentional.

Ben & Jerry's did not try to control perception. They honored identity. That distinction preserved trust among those who had always understood the brand to stand for something beyond profit.

What These Two Stories Reveal

United and Ben & Jerry's offer a stark contrast. United spoke procedurally when the moment demanded humanity. Ben & Jerry's spoke morally when neutrality would have been easier.

One sounded surprised by public reaction. The other accepted consequence as part of representation.

This is the thread that runs through institutional trust. Institutions do not lose trust because they take positions. They lose trust because they appear unmoored from their own values.

The Three Duties of Institutional Voice

When your voice represents more than you, there are three duties you must honor, every time.

1. Duty of Care
Your words should not create new harm.

No unnecessary details that expose victims.
No speculation that becomes accusation.
No "clarity" that retraumatizes the people harmed.

Care is not softness.

It is protection.

2. Duty of Truth

Your words should not create false safety.

Truth is not only accuracy. It is alignment between what you know, what you say, and what people experience.

If you do not know, say you do not know.
If facts are changing, say they are changing.
If an investigation is ongoing, give timing and process.

Truth stabilizes because it limits imagination.

3. Duty of Dignity

Your words must preserve humanity, even when someone is angry, when the institution is criticized, and when you are afraid.

Dignity is the refusal to talk about people like problems. It is the refusal to reduce harm to procedure.

This is the difference between saying, "We are reviewing protocols," and saying, "We know people were hurt, and we take that seriously."

Institutional Voice and the Discipline of C.A.L.M.

C.A.L.M. is not only a framework for individual leaders. It is an institutional discipline.

Centering requires leaders to decenter ego and urgency. Acknowledgment requires naming harm without hedging. Leading with facts requires sequencing truth to stabilize meaning. Modeling accountability requires staying present long after attention fades.

Most institutions fail not in the first response, but in the sustained one. Accountability that disappears feels transactional. Accountability that endures feels trustworthy.

This is why C.A.L.M. is not a one-time performance. It is a standard of conduct.

The Shift From Story to Stewardship

Chapter 7 was about owning your story. Chapter 8 is about recognizing when the story is no longer yours alone.

When you speak for an institution, your voice becomes a vessel. It carries people who may never get the microphone. It carries history you did not create. It carries consequences you must still own.

Leadership at this level is not about sounding good. It is about sounding aligned.

Because when the spotlight is hot and silence would be easier, people are not asking whether you are eloquent. They are asking whether you understand the weight of being heard.

Where We Go Next

In the next chapter, we move from responsibility to application.

We will take C.A.L.M. into real-world scenarios where leaders are tested not by belief, but by execution: corporate crises, government emergencies, public scrutiny, incomplete information, and high emotion.

Because leadership is not proven in theory. It is proven in moments.

And the leaders who endure are the ones who understand this. Your voice carries others. Your silence speaks loudly. And when you represent more than yourself, calm is not optional.

It is essential.

Speaking for Institutions, Not Just Yourself

When you speak for an institution, your voice becomes a vessel.

It carries people who do not have access to microphones, cameras, or press briefings. It carries history you did not create. It carries consequences you must still own.

This chapter established a critical truth of advanced leadership communication:

**Institutional voice is not about self-expression.
It is about stewardship.**

Leaders lose trust not because they speak, but because they speak without alignment. They default to neutrality when moral clarity is required. They protect the institution's image instead of the people it serves. They explain policy before acknowledging harm. And in doing so, they surrender meaning.

Institutional trust is built when leaders understand that:

- Silence is interpreted, not neutral
- Timing shapes meaning as much as content
- Values must be audible before procedures
- Accountability must endure, not perform

When institutional voice is disciplined, people may disagree with decisions—but they do not feel erased by them.

The Institutional C.A.L.M. Checklist

Use this checklist **before**, **during**, and **after** any moment where you are speaking on behalf of an institution.

This is not a messaging tool.
It is a leadership discipline.

C — Center the Institution Before You Speak

Before issuing any statement, ask:

- Are we reacting from fear, or responding from responsibility?
- Is urgency being driven by headlines or by harm?
- Are we regulating internally before communicating externally?
- Have decision-makers slowed down enough to think clearly?

If leadership is internally escalated, institutional language will leak defensiveness.

Do not speak until the institution is regulated enough to be steady.

A — Acknowledge Harm Before Explaining Policy

Before facts, procedures, or legal framing:

- Have we named what people are feeling?
- Have we acknowledged impact without minimizing it?
- Have we spoken to human experience before institutional process?

- Have we avoided language that sounds clinical, distant, or dismissive?

If people do not feel seen, they will not hear what comes next.

Acknowledgment is not liability.
It is containment.

L — Lead With Facts That Stabilize Meaning

When facts are incomplete, discipline matters more than certainty.

Confirm:

- Are we clearly separating what we know from what we do not?
- Are we avoiding speculation, euphemisms, or reassurance language?
- Are facts being used to inform, not defend?
- Are we providing a clear cadence for updates?

Facts should limit fear—not inflame it.

Clarity builds trust when certainty is unavailable.

M — Model Accountability Beyond the Moment

After the statement is issued, leadership responsibility increases.

Ask:

- Are leaders remaining visible after attention fades?
- Are actions aligning with stated values?
- Are updates consistent, even when progress is slow?

- Are we correcting misinformation quickly and publicly?
- Are we protecting dignity in what we do next—not just what we said first?

Accountability is not proven in statements.

It is proven in sustained presence.

The Final Test of Institutional Voice

Before any public communication, answer this question honestly:

Does this protect the people we serve—or does it protect us?

If the answer is unclear, stop.

That pause is leadership.

Looking Ahead

Chapter 9 moves from principle to execution.

We will apply C.A.L.M. to real-world leadership scenarios:

- Corporate crises
- Government emergencies
- Public backlash
- Incomplete information
- High-emotion environments

Because leadership is not proven by belief.

It is proven by behavior.

And when you speak for institutions, calm is not optional.

It is essential.

PART IV:
APPLICATION AND LEGACY

Chapter 9
Leadership Without Certainty

How leaders steady others when the facts are incomplete

Before You Read On

This chapter is designed to be applied, not just absorbed.

Because leadership without certainty cannot be mastered through observation alone, I've created a **free companion workbook** for Chapter 9 to help you work through the principles, scenarios, and decisions explored here in real time.

You can download the workbook at:

www.dionnasmith.com/workbook

The exercises are designed to help you:

- Identify how you personally respond under pressure
- Practice applying the C.A.L.M. framework to real-world leadership moments
- Prepare for situations where clarity is incomplete but leadership is required

Many readers choose to read this chapter once, then return with the workbook to deepen the work.

When the Moment Will Not Wait

Every leader eventually encounters a moment that does not wait for preparation. It does not arrive neatly packaged with confirmed facts, aligned advisors, or a clear communications plan. It arrives fractured, emotional, public, and urgent.

A video goes viral before anyone can verify what happened. An employee is harmed or lost before leadership has language for the grief. An allegation surfaces that cuts directly against an organization's stated values. A candidate or elected official is thrust into scrutiny where every word will be interpreted as strategy.

These moments share one defining characteristic:

They demand leadership before certainty exists.

This is where many leaders freeze.

They believe leadership begins after clarity arrives. They wait for confirmation, for investigation, for legal review. But crisis does not wait. And leadership that waits too long is often indistinguishable from avoidance.

The most damaging leadership failures do not occur because leaders lacked information. They occur because leaders allowed uncertainty to override empathy, urgency to override judgment, or fear to override presence.

This chapter exists for those moments.

It is not about perfect statements. It is not about clever messaging. It is not about winning the news cycle. It is about how leaders show up when answers are incomplete and consequences are real.

Across government, corporate, nonprofit, and political leadership, the contexts differ, but the expectations do not.

People want to know: do you see what is happening? Do you understand why it matters? Can we trust you to lead us through it?

This is where C.A.L.M. becomes operational.

Leadership Begins Before You Speak

Before any statement is drafted, before any spokesperson is prepped, before any press release is approved, leadership must do something that feels counterintuitive under pressure: slow down.

The first job of leadership is not response. It is regulation.

When panic enters the room, it multiplies. When urgency replaces judgment, mistakes follow. When language is released too quickly, it cannot be retrieved.

Centering is the discipline of stabilizing yourself and your leadership team before attempting to stabilize anyone else. Who needs to be in the room right now? Who is adding clarity, and who is adding noise? What do we actually know, and what are we assuming?

Centering is not delay. It is discipline. Only regulated leaders can regulate moments.

Acknowledgment Before Answers

Once leaders center themselves, the next instinct is often to explain. Explanation feels productive. Explanation feels intelligent. Explanation feels safer than emotion.

But explanation without acknowledgment feels cold.

Acknowledgment is not an admission of guilt. It is recognition of impact.

People do not need conclusions in the early moments of crisis. They need to feel seen.

Acknowledgment sounds like this: we are aware. We understand why this is concerning. We are taking this seriously.

Without acknowledgment, facts will not land. Without acknowledgment, accuracy feels dismissive.

Facts as Anchors, Not Shields

Facts matter. Truth matters. Accuracy matters.

But facts delivered without care can escalate harm.

Leading with facts responsibly means sequencing truth in a way that stabilizes rather than shuts down conversation. Here is what we know so far. Here is what we are still learning. Here is what we are committed to sharing as more becomes clear.

Facts should anchor the moment, not shield leadership from responsibility.

Accountability Is a Posture, Not a Statement

Accountability is not a press release. It is not a single appearance. It is not a carefully worded paragraph.

Accountability is sustained presence.

It is staying visible while facts unfold. It is communicating even when there is nothing new to report. It is reaffirming values while outcomes remain uncertain.

This is where trust is either preserved or lost.

As you read the scenarios that follow, you may find it helpful to pause and reflect on how you would respond in each moment. The Chapter 9 companion workbook includes guided prompts to support this reflection and can be accessed at:

www.dionnasmith.com/workbook

A Note on the Scenarios

The scenarios that follow are informed by real-world leadership and communications challenges commonly faced across corporate, government, nonprofit, and political institutions. They are composite examples designed to illustrate patterns, principles, and best practices—not accounts of any specific organization, incident, or jurisdiction.

References to leadership responses, institutional behavior, or outcomes are generalized and anonymized. These scenarios should not be interpreted as descriptions of events involving any particular employer, agency, or government entity.

Scenario One: When a Public Safety Incident Goes Viral

(Government Leadership)

The moment rarely arrives with warning.

A video appears online. Shaky. Incomplete. Charged. Within minutes, it is everywhere.

A public interaction involving an authority figure has been captured on a phone and shared without context. The footage is disturbing enough to spark outrage, but unclear enough to invite speculation. Commentators fill the gaps immediately. Headlines follow. Pressure mounts.

Inside the institution, leaders scramble. Phones ring. Advisors speak over one another. Someone asks, "Do we know what actually happened?" Someone else responds, "We can't say anything until we confirm the facts."

This is the moment when leadership is most likely to fail. Not because leaders are malicious or incompetent, but because uncertainty triggers instinct. And instinct is rarely strategic.

The Wrong Instinct

The most common instinct in this moment takes one of three forms: silence, defensiveness, or procedure.

Silence feels safe because it avoids saying the wrong thing. Defensiveness feels necessary because the institution feels attacked. Procedure feels responsible because it sounds official.

All three instincts are understandable. All three are damaging.

Silence communicates indifference. Defensiveness signals alignment with harm. Procedure sounds like evasion.

The public is not waiting for certainty. They are waiting for acknowledgment. Leadership does not require answers in this moment. It requires presence.

Center: Regulating the Room Before Speaking

Before any statement is drafted, leadership must center. This means slowing the room down, not to delay action, but to prevent panic from dictating posture.

Who needs to be in the room right now? Who is adding clarity, and who is escalating fear? What decisions must be made immediately, and which can wait?

Centering is active containment. It is the leader saying, we will not rush into language we cannot stand behind. Because once words are released, they cannot be retrieved.

Acknowledge: Naming What People Are Experiencing

Acknowledgment is not an admission of guilt. It is recognition of reality.

In this scenario, acknowledgment sounds like this: we are aware of the video circulating. We understand why it is concerning. We take incidents involving public safety seriously. We are working to gather all relevant information.

It does not speculate. It does not defend. It does not explain. It signals awareness, concern, and responsibility.

Lead With Facts: Using Truth as an Anchor, Not a Shield

As information emerges, leaders must resist the urge to weaponize facts. Facts should stabilize the moment, not shut it down.

Here is what we know so far. Here is what we are still determining. Here is what we will share when we know more.

Facts should follow acknowledgment, not replace it.

Model Accountability: Staying Present While the Story Unfolds

Accountability here does not mean assigning blame prematurely. It means staying visible. It means continuing to communicate even when there is nothing new to report. It means reaffirming values while facts are still emerging.

This is where many institutions fail. They issue one statement and then disappear. The investigation continues quietly. The public fills the silence loudly.

Accountability is not a press release. It is a posture.

C.A.L.M. in Action

Center by regulating the room before speaking. Acknowledge harm without speculation or defensiveness. Lead with facts as they emerge, not as shields. Model accountability by staying present beyond the headline.

In public leadership, credibility is not built by speed. It is built by steadiness.

Scenario Two: When an Employee Is Seriously Harmed or Dies

(Corporate Leadership)

The call comes early.

An employee has been critically injured, or worse, during the workday. Details are still emerging. Leadership is informed before most of the organization knows, but word is already spreading.

Slack messages pause mid-sentence. Emails go unanswered. Managers do not know what to say to their teams. Executives are ushered into emergency meetings.

Inside the organization, shock sets in. Outside the organization, questions begin forming.

Was this preventable?
Was safety ignored?
Who is responsible?

This is one of the most difficult leadership moments any organization will face, because the stakes are human before they are reputational. And yet, this is where institutions most often sound inhuman.

The Wrong Instinct

In moments of workplace harm or death, institutional instinct almost always leans toward legal protection. Counsel advises caution. Human resources advises minimal language. Executives fear liability.

The result is often a statement that sounds like this: "We are aware of an incident involving an employee. An investigation is underway."

It is accurate. It is defensible. It is devastating.

To the people inside the organization and the public watching, it sounds like indifference. The wrong instinct here is to treat this moment as a risk-management issue first and a human moment second. That order matters.

Center: Creating Space for Humanity Before Protocol

Before drafting any statement, leadership must center the organization. This is not about speed. It is about posture.

Centering in this scenario means pausing to acknowledge what has happened internally before speaking externally. Who has been notified personally? Who is supporting the employee's family? What do frontline managers need right now?

Centering also means slowing the leadership team down. This is not the moment to debate phrasing endlessly or outsource emotion to a press release. This is the moment to decide who the organization is going to be in the face of loss.

Leadership must signal clearly: we will not allow process to eclipse people.

Acknowledge: Naming Loss Without Legal Panic

Acknowledgment here is not an admission of fault. It is recognition of humanity.

In this scenario, acknowledgment sounds like this: we are heartbroken by what has occurred. Our thoughts are with the employee and their loved ones. This loss matters to us.

It centers the human impact. It communicates care without speculation. It affirms values before outcomes.

Leaders often fear this step. They worry empathy will be construed as liability. But the absence of empathy creates its own risk, one that no legal review can repair.

People do not need answers yet. They need acknowledgment.

Lead With Facts: What to Say When You Know Very Little

Facts in this scenario are often sparse. The instinct is either to say too much or nothing at all.

C.A.L.M. teaches a different approach.

Leaders should say: here is what we know at this time. Here is what we are still learning. Here is what we are committed to understanding fully.

This frames facts as a process, not a defense. It reassures employees and the public that leadership is engaged, not evasive. Facts should be shared with care, and always after acknowledgment, not instead of it.

Model Accountability: Staying Present After the Moment Passes

This is where most organizations fail.

They issue a statement. They express condolences. They move on.

But employees do not move on. Families do not move on. Communities do not move on.

Modeling accountability here means staying present long after attention fades. It means communicating outcomes of investigations. It means naming changes being made. It means honoring the person lost, not just managing the event.

Accountability is not closure. It is continuity.

When organizations disappear after tragedy, they teach people that care was temporary. When leaders stay present, they rebuild trust slowly, visibly, and honestly.

The Leadership Lesson

In moments of workplace harm or death, leaders are not judged by how well they protect the organization. They are judged by how well they honor humanity.

People do not expect perfection. They expect decency.

Leadership without certainty in this scenario means resisting the urge to hide behind protocol and choosing to lead with care, clarity, and consistency.

This is what C.A.L.M. looks like when the stakes are human.

When leaders center people, they steady grief. When they acknowledge loss, they preserve dignity. When they lead with facts responsibly, they build credibility. When they model accountability over time, they rebuild trust.

In moments like this, leaders do not transmit certainty. They transmit care.

And care, in times of loss, is leadership.

C.A.L.M. in Action

Center by prioritizing people before protocol and regulating the organization before responding publicly.
Acknowledge loss with humanity, without legal panic or speculation.
Lead with facts carefully, naming what is known and unknown without over-explaining.
Model accountability through sustained presence, transparency, and follow-through.

In moments of workplace tragedy, leadership is not measured by precision.

It is measured by care.

Scenario Three: When a Mission-Driven Organization Faces Allegations

(Nonprofit Leadership)

The call does not come from the media first. It comes from inside the organization.

A staff member sends a message late at night. A board member forwards an email marked urgent. A donor asks a careful question that feels heavier than it looks.

An allegation has surfaced.

It may involve misconduct, discrimination, misuse of funds, or behavior that directly contradicts the organization's stated values. The details are incomplete. The source is unclear. But the potential damage is undeniable.

For mission-driven organizations, this moment cuts deeper than most, because credibility is not just reputational. It is existential.

Why This Moment Is Uniquely Dangerous

Nonprofits are built on trust. Donors give because they believe. Communities engage because they trust. Staff stay because they feel aligned with the mission.

When allegations surface, leaders feel the ground shift beneath them. The instinct is to protect the mission at all costs. And that instinct is precisely what can destroy it.

The Wrong Instinct

In this moment, nonprofit leaders often default to one of three responses: defensiveness disguised as righteousness, silence framed as discretion, or over-performing values instead of addressing harm.

The language sounds like this: "This does not reflect who we are." "We take these accusations very seriously." "We remain committed to our mission."

These statements are not false, but they are insufficient. They speak about the organization instead of to the concern.

The public hears deflection. Staff hear avoidance. Communities hear dismissal.

The wrong instinct is to defend the mission before tending to the moment.

Center: Separating Identity from Accountability

Before anything is said publicly, leadership must center, and that requires discipline.

Centering here means resisting the urge to collapse identity into defense. The organization's mission may be good. Its impact may be real. Its history may be strong. None of that negates the need for accountability.

Leadership must slow the room down and ask: what exactly has been raised? Who is impacted right now? What does safety look like for staff, volunteers, and community members?

Centering also requires leaders to resist pressure from donors, board members, or advisors who want the issue contained quickly.

This is not a containment moment. It is a credibility moment.

Acknowledge: Naming the Moment Without Performing Innocence

Acknowledgment is where nonprofit leaders most often fail. They rush to reassure instead of recognizing.

In this scenario, acknowledgment sounds like this: we are aware of the concerns that have been raised. We understand why these allegations are serious. We are committed to addressing them with care and transparency.

This does not deny. It does not confirm. It does not posture. It affirms that the organization understands the gravity of the moment.

Acknowledgment here is not about optics. It is about trust.

People want to know whether leadership is listening, not whether it is persuasive.

Lead With Facts: Allowing Process Without Hiding Behind It

Nonprofit leaders often hide behind process in moments like this. They say, "An investigation is underway," and then retreat into silence.

Process matters. But process without communication feels evasive.

Leading with facts responsibly means explaining how the organization is responding without over-promising outcomes. This sounds like: here is what we are doing to understand the situation. Here is who is involved in that process. Here is how we will share information as it becomes available.

Facts should clarify commitment, not close conversation. They must always follow acknowledgment, not replace it.

Model Accountability: Staying Visible When Trust Is Tested

This is the moment when leadership posture matters more than messaging.

Accountability here means staying visible, not disappearing behind the board, legal counsel, or internal review. It means checking in with staff, not just issuing statements. It means communicating with donors without spin. It means affirming values through action, not slogans.

Most importantly, it means being willing to confront uncomfortable truths, even if they complicate the organization's narrative.

Nonprofits lose trust not because they are imperfect, but because they protect reputation at the expense of people.

Accountability is demonstrated through consistency, transparency, and follow-through.

The Leadership Lesson

When allegations surface in mission-driven organizations, leaders are not judged by how passionately they defend their values. They are judged by whether they live them.

Leadership without certainty in this scenario requires humility. It requires leaders to say: we may not know everything yet, but we are committed to knowing more and to doing what is right, not what is convenient.

When leaders center before responding, they preserve integrity. When they acknowledge without defensiveness, they protect trust. When they lead with facts responsibly, they sustain credibility. When they model accountability over time, they honor the mission.

In moments like this, leaders do not transmit certainty. They transmit integrity.

And integrity, especially when tested, is the true measure of leadership.

CALM in Action

Center by separating the mission from the moment and slowing the organization before responding publicly.
Acknowledge the seriousness of concerns without denial, defensiveness, or performance.
Lead with facts by explaining process clearly while avoiding silence or over-promising.
Model accountability through visibility, transparency, and follow-through — even when the truth is uncomfortable.

In mission-driven organizations, values are not proven by what is stated.

They are proven by what leaders do when those values are tested.

Scenario Four: When a Candidate or Elected Official Is Suddenly Under Scrutiny

(Political Leadership)

The moment does not feel hypothetical. It feels personal.

A comment resurfaces. A decision is questioned. An allegation emerges, amplified by a headline, a clip, or a post stripped of context and shared at speed.

For a candidate running for office or an elected official already in public service, the scrutiny is immediate and unforgiving. Advisors flood the inbox. Opponents weigh in publicly. Supporters demand reassurance. Critics demand accountability.

The pressure is relentless.

And unlike other leadership contexts, politics adds one destabilizing element: every response will be interpreted as strategy.

This is where leadership most often collapses into performance.

Why This Moment Is Uniquely Volatile

Political leadership operates in a permanent spotlight. Intent is questioned. Motives are assumed. Silence is framed as guilt.

Acknowledgment is framed as weakness. Explanation is framed as spin.

There is no neutral ground.

Candidates and elected officials feel compelled to respond quickly, not because it is wise, but because delay is weaponized. This creates a dangerous reflex: message before meaning.

When that happens, leadership disappears and optics take over.

The Wrong Instinct

The most common instinct in this moment is spin.

Talking points are drafted immediately. Language is softened. Responsibility is reframed. Advisors focus on winning the news cycle instead of stewarding trust.

The statements sound like this: "This is a distraction." "My record speaks for itself." "This is being taken out of context."

These responses may rally supporters, but they deepen public skepticism. People are not listening for positioning. They are listening for authenticity.

The wrong instinct here is to treat the moment as a communications problem instead of a leadership test.

Center: Choosing Leadership Over Optics

Before speaking, political leaders must center, and this is harder than it sounds.

Centering in this context means resisting the urge to respond solely for advantage. It means slowing the internal frenzy and grounding decisions in values rather than polls.

The questions leaders must ask are not: how do we neutralize this, or how do we survive the cycle.

They are: what responsibility do I hold in this moment, what does leadership look like beyond messaging, and what would credibility require if no cameras were present.

Centering is the discipline of choosing leadership over performance, even when performance would be easier.

Acknowledge: Speaking Without Performing Innocence

Acknowledgment is the most fragile step in political leadership.

Candidates and elected officials often fear that acknowledgment will be perceived as admission or weakness. But avoidance communicates something far worse: calculation.

In this scenario, acknowledgment sounds like this: I am aware of the concerns that have been raised. I understand why people are asking questions. This matters, and it deserves to be addressed thoughtfully.

This does not concede facts prematurely. It does not attack critics. It does not redirect blame.

It establishes seriousness.

Acknowledgment signals that the leader understands the weight of public trust and is not hiding behind defensiveness or distraction.

Lead With Facts: Resisting the Urge to Over-Explain

Political leaders often fall into one of two traps when facts are incomplete. They over-explain, or they deny entirely.

Both approaches erode trust.

Leading with facts responsibly means separating what is known from what is still being examined, without speculation, minimization, or attack.

This sounds like: here is what I know at this time. Here is what I am still reviewing. Here is what I am committed to clarifying fully.

Facts should clarify posture, not posture as proof.

When leaders use facts as shields, credibility erodes. When they use facts as anchors, trust stabilizes.

Model Accountability: Staying Present Beyond the News Cycle

This is where political leadership is most often exposed.

The first statement goes out. The headlines shift. And the leader disappears.

Accountability does not end when coverage fades.

Modeling accountability in this scenario means staying present even when it is uncomfortable, continuing to address questions, clarifying positions, and demonstrating consistency between words and actions.

It means allowing the public to see growth, learning, or correction if warranted, not because it polls well, but because it is honest.

Accountability is not weakness in political leadership. It is credibility.

The Leadership Lesson

When candidates or elected officials come under scrutiny, they are not judged by whether they avoid criticism.

They are judged by whether they can be trusted with power.

Leadership without certainty in this scenario requires courage.

The courage to resist spin.
The courage to speak without full resolution.
The courage to prioritize integrity over advantage.

When leaders center before responding, they regain control.
When they acknowledge concern without defensiveness, they preserve trust.
When they lead with facts responsibly, they demonstrate seriousness.
When they model accountability over time, they earn credibility.

In moments like this, leaders do not transmit certainty.

They transmit character.

And in political leadership, character — more than charisma, more than strategy, more than messaging — is what endures.

CALM in Action

Center by choosing leadership over optics and grounding decisions in values rather than polls.
Acknowledge concern without defensiveness or performance.

Lead with facts without over-explaining, denying prematurely, or weaponizing information.
Model accountability by staying present beyond the news cycle and allowing credibility to be rebuilt through consistency.

In political leadership, credibility is not built through perfection.

It is built through consistency.

What Leaders Get Wrong Under Pressure

Across sectors, the failures are predictable. Leaders over-explain. They defend too early. They outsource empathy to statements. They disappear after the first response.

These are not moral failures. They are timing failures.

C.A.L.M. exists to interrupt these instincts.

From Crisis to Credibility

Crisis does not automatically destroy trust. Avoidance does.

When leaders show up with care, clarity, and consistency, even without certainty, they stabilize their institutions. They remind people that leadership is not about having all the answers. It is about how you hold responsibility while seeking them.

Closing: Calm Is Contagious

Leaders do not transmit certainty. They transmit calm.

When leaders regulate themselves, they steady others. When they acknowledge impact, they preserve trust. When they stay present, they demonstrate integrity.

This is leadership without certainty. And it is often leadership at its most powerful.

From the Moment to the Meaning

The scenarios in this chapter are not rare. They are inevitable.

Every leader, regardless of sector, title, or tenure, will face moments where the facts are incomplete, the pressure is public, and the consequences are real. What separates effective leaders from damaging ones is not preparation alone, but posture.

Across government, corporate, nonprofit, and political leadership, the pattern is clear. When leaders rush, trust fractures. When leaders defend, credibility erodes. When leaders disappear, fear fills the void.

But when leaders center themselves, acknowledge impact, lead with facts responsibly, and model accountability over time, something stabilizing happens. People breathe.

C.A.L.M. is not a communications tactic for crisis moments only. It is a leadership discipline that shapes how institutions show up, not just when things go wrong, but every day in between.

The true test of leadership is not whether you can respond in a moment of disruption. It is whether the way you lead in those moments reflects who you claim to be when things are calm.

C.A.L.M. is not a theory to admire.
It is a discipline to practice.

To support your leadership beyond these pages, I've created a **free Chapter 9 workbook** that translates the ideas, scenarios, and lessons in this chapter into practical reflection and application.

You can download it at:

www.dionnasmith.com/workbook

The workbook will help you:

- Apply C.A.L.M. to moments you've already lived through
- Prepare for moments you have not yet faced
- Clarify how you want to show up when leadership is required before certainty arrives

Leadership is not proven by what we understand.
It is proven by what we practice under pressure.

In the next chapter, we move beyond the moment itself. We will explore how leaders embed C.A.L.M. into their organizations, teams, and cultures so that steadiness is not improvised under pressure, but practiced long before it is needed.

Because the goal is not just to survive the moment. It is to become the kind of leader, and build the kind of institution, that people trust before the next one arrives.

Chapter 10
When It Matters Most

"There will always be reasons to wait.
Leadership begins when you choose not to."
— *On the Record*

There are moments that do not announce themselves as turning points until long after they have passed. At the time, they feel like chaos, like urgency, like survival. Only later do they reveal themselves as teachers.

When I look back across my life and career, I can trace my understanding of leadership communication not to classrooms or credentials, but to crises. Moments when words were scarce, stakes were high, and silence carried consequences. Moments when communication did not simply shape perception, but altered outcomes. Moments when the absence of clarity multiplied harm and the presence of calm made space for healing.

This chapter is not a conclusion. It is a reckoning.

A reckoning with what I learned when systems failed. With what I witnessed when leaders rose or disappeared. With why I believe, with conviction earned the hard way, that communication is not an accessory to leadership. It is leadership.

And when it matters most, it is the difference between escalation and stability, between fracture and trust, between loss and meaning.

When pressure hits, communication is not what you do after leadership. It is how leadership shows up.

Katrina: When Silence Became a Sentence

Hurricane Katrina did not only devastate a city. It exposed a leadership vacuum.

In the days after the storm, as New Orleans drowned under water and neglect, what people needed most was not reassurance. They needed acknowledgment. They needed leadership that could name the disaster honestly, speak with urgency, and coordinate action visibly.

Instead, they received delay, confusion, and contradiction.

Information trickled instead of flowing. Press conferences replaced presence. Officials spoke around the suffering instead of to the people living inside it.

And the silence, especially from those with the greatest power, became its own form of violence.

I watched people plead not just for rescue, but for recognition. They were stranded not only physically, but narratively. Their reality was not being told accurately or forcefully by those entrusted with authority. The world saw fragments. The people living it felt erased.

What Katrina taught me, before I had language for it, was this. When leaders fail to communicate clearly in crisis, they do not simply lose trust. They compound harm.

I learned that leadership is not proven by what you know, but by what you are willing to say when the truth is uncomfortable and the optics are unforgiving. I learned that speed without clarity breeds chaos, and silence without empathy feels like abandonment.

Most of all, I learned that communication is never neutral. It either steadies people or destabilizes them.

Corporate Crisis: COVID, George Floyd, and the Weight of Words

Years later, I found myself inside boardrooms and crisis rooms during two of the most destabilizing moments modern corporate leadership has faced: the COVID-19 pandemic and the murder of George Floyd.

Executives were not prepared. Not because they were incompetent, but because they had never been required to lead publicly through grief, fear, moral reckoning, and uncertainty all at once.

COVID stripped away the illusion of control. Leaders were forced to speak without answers, to reassure without certainty, to lead workforces scattered across kitchen tables and hospital beds. Every message carried anxiety. Every pause felt ominous.

Then George Floyd stripped away something deeper: neutrality.

Suddenly, statements were no longer optional. Silence was interpreted as complicity. Employees wanted to know where their leaders stood, not in theory, but in humanity.

I watched leaders freeze, draft, redraft, and delay. I watched legal caution eclipse moral clarity. I watched statements that said nothing precisely because they were written to offend no one.

And I watched employees disengage, not because perfection was missing, but because courage was.

But I also witnessed something else.

I saw leaders who chose to speak honestly instead of safely. Who acknowledged pain before explaining policy. Who admitted uncertainty without retreating from responsibility. Who showed up consistently, not just once, but repeatedly.

Those leaders stabilized their organizations. Not because they got everything right, but because they communicated with integrity.

From those moments, I learned that great communication does not eliminate crisis. It contains it.

Public Service: When Words Carry Weight You Cannot Undo

Nothing, however, prepared me for the shift into public service.

In government, communication is no longer transactional. It is existential. You are not speaking to customers who can leave or employees who can resign. You are speaking to residents who must live with the consequences of every word, every delay, every omission.

In public service, people are not listening for polish. They are listening for safety.

I learned quickly that messaging failures in government are not reputational inconveniences. They are lived experiences. When communication breaks down, fear fills the vacuum. When leaders speak abstractly, people feel dismissed. When institutions retreat into silence, communities feel betrayed.

Serving in public leadership taught me that communication is not about defending systems. It is about protecting people.

It also taught me that words do not disappear once spoken. They echo. They are replayed. They are quoted, misinterpreted, and remembered.

That reality forces a different discipline. A deeper one.

You must center yourself before you speak. You must acknowledge before you explain. You must lead with facts responsibly. And you must remain accountable long after the cameras leave.

This is not theory. This is survival.

What I Know Now

After decades of watching leaders succeed and fail in moments that mattered most, one truth has become undeniable.

Great communication does not come from talent. It comes from intention.

It is not about eloquence. It is about alignment.

It is not about controlling narrative. It is about stewarding trust.

I have seen calm language de-escalate volatile situations. I have seen thoughtful statements slow misinformation. I have seen leaders recover credibility not by perfection, but by presence.

And I have seen the opposite.

I have seen poorly chosen words inflame grief. I have seen silence deepen suspicion. I have seen leaders lose authority not because of what happened, but because of how they spoke when it did.

This is why I teach communication the way I do. Not as performance. Not as branding. Not as spin. But as leadership discipline.

C.A.L.M. as Practice, Not Performance

C.A.L.M. was not created in a conference room. It emerged from watching what worked when everything else failed.

Centering is not about composure. It is about regulation. Leaders must steady themselves before they can steady others.

Acknowledgment is not admission. It is recognition. People need to know they are seen before they can hear what comes next.

Leading with facts is not about defense. It is about anchoring truth without weaponizing it.

Modeling accountability is not about punishment. It is about presence over time.

When used properly, C.A.L.M. does not eliminate uncertainty. It makes uncertainty survivable.

It teaches leaders how to speak without certainty and still be trusted. How to hold power without losing empathy. How to tell the truth without inflaming fear. How to remain present when retreat would be easier.

I have watched leaders apply C.A.L.M. and change the temperature of rooms, organizations, and communities, not because the situation disappeared, but because panic did.

And here is what I want to make plain.

C.A.L.M. is not only for crises that make headlines. It is for the meeting where your team is scared to tell you the truth. It is for the moment your employee breaks down and does not know how to keep going. It is for the community outrage you feel tempted to dismiss because it feels unfair. It is for the board conversation where everyone wants to protect the institution more than the people.

C.A.L.M. is not reserved for catastrophe. It is the way you become the kind of leader people can trust before catastrophe arrives.

CALM in the Moment: A Leadership Protocol

When the pressure hits and time feels compressed, leaders do not need more language.
They need an anchor.

Here is the CALM protocol as it lives in real time:

First, Center.
Pause before you speak. Regulate yourself and the room. Ask what is known, what is assumed, and who needs to be present. Decide what you will not do—panic, posture, perform.

Second, Acknowledge.
Name what people are experiencing. Fear, grief, confusion, anger. Recognition must come before explanation. If people feel unseen, nothing you say will feel true.

Third, Lead with Facts.
Share what is known. Name what is unknown. Commit to when and how updates will come. Use truth as an anchor—not a shield.

Fourth, Model Accountability.
Stay visible. Follow through. Let actions confirm words. Do not disappear once the statement is issued. The "day after" is where trust is decided.

This sequence does not make leadership easy.
It makes it credible.

The Work After the Book

If you have read this far, you are not looking for communication tricks.

You are looking for leadership that holds.

So here is what I want you to do—practically, immediately.

Build your CALM readiness before you need it.

- Write your **non-negotiables** now, while you are calm.
  What will you never do to protect image?
  What do you owe the people you serve?
  What does dignity require from you?
- Decide your **cadence** now.
  When the next crisis comes, you will not rise to the occasion—you will default to your training.
  Choose your rhythm before panic chooses it for you.
- Prepare your **first three sentences** now.
  The first credible frame usually wins.
  What will you say when you don't know everything yet?
  Practice the language of honesty *without* speculation.

- Commit to **visibility** now.
  Do not promise yourself you will stay present and then vanish when it gets loud.
  Decide ahead of time: I will not delegate the hardest moment.

This is what strong leaders do differently.

They do not wait until the fire to decide who they are.
They decide while things are quiet.

Why This Work Matters

I am committed to helping leaders communicate when it matters most because I have seen what happens when they do not. I have lived the cost of silence. I have witnessed the power of clarity. I have seen how the right words, delivered at the right time and with the right posture, can change trajectories. This work is not about speaking louder. It is about speaking truer. It is about understanding that leadership is not proven in calm seasons, but in storms. And storms are coming. They always do.

If you take nothing else from this book, take this truth with you. Your voice is not accidental. Your silence is not neutral. And your words will outlive the moment in which they are spoken. When pressure arrives, leaders do not get to opt out of meaning. They either shape it with intention or surrender it to fear, speculation, and noise.

So when the moment comes, make a vow to yourself. Center before the noise takes over. Acknowledge truth before fear fills the silence. Lead with facts that steady rather than shatter. Model accountability long after attention fades. Choose calm over chaos. Choose clarity over comfort. Choose leadership over delay. Remember that presence is power.

Leadership is not measured by titles held or statements issued. It is measured by how people feel after hearing you speak. It is measured by whether trust grows or fractures, by whether calm spreads or fear does. You do not need perfection. You need presence. You do not need certainty. You need integrity.

When the moment comes, remember this. Calm is not weakness. Clarity is not cruelty. Accountability is not optional. It is leadership. And when it matters most, it is everything.

Be the calm. Someone is watching you, not to see if you are flawless, but to see if they are safe. You do not lead by having all the answers. You lead by how you hold people while you seek them. Calm is not what you say. It is what people feel after you speak.

Be the calm.

EPILOGUE
When the Voice Outlives the Words

"Jesus wept."
"If not now, then when."

Two sentences raised me. Two benedictions built me. And in the end, two women who spoke until speech itself slipped away.

I did not notice the silence at first. It came softly, the way night comes, one lamp at a time going dark. A name misplaced. A story told out of order. A pause that lingered too long between thought and sound. Then, as seasons turned, silence settled in my grandmothers' homes like new and uninvited furniture.

Ida, whose kitchen could feed a neighborhood and a broken heart in the same afternoon, began searching for simple words that once came easily. The recipes stayed in her hands, but the measurements slipped from her tongue. Where there had been sentences, there were hums. Where there had been directives, there were smiles. Her eyes still knew us, but the stories that stitched us together loosened their threads.

Roxie, whose porch ran on power and purpose, began to misplace the details of the movements she led. The clipboard became a coaster. The voter rolls turned into paper for shopping lists. And yet, even as language thinned, her spirit stayed loud. Some mornings she would rock and whisper her one remaining liturgy to the quiet room, "Jesus wept," until the sound felt like a prayer strong enough to hold the world.

Dementia is a thief with soft shoes. It does not slam doors. It steals the hinges. It does not empty a life in a single night. It turns down the volume until you have to put your ear against the past to hear it. I watched the women who taught me to speak become women whose mouths forgot the routes their hearts still knew. It was the cruelest irony I have ever witnessed. My first and finest teachers in communication silenced by a disease that unthreads the sentence from the soul.

But here is the mystery that changed me. Even when their words faded, their message did not. The kitchen still gathered people. The porch still expected courage. The rooms still remembered their rhythms. Love left a resonance. What they had repeated for decades became muscle memory in us.

I carry that lesson into every briefing room and boardroom. When I tell leaders that communication is a form of leadership, I am not only talking about microphones and media. I am talking about legacy. About building a cadence so consistent that even when your voice falls quiet, your values keep speaking.

Ida's last vocabulary was presence. She sat. She hummed. She held your hand longer than necessary, as if to say, you are not alone. Roxie's final sermon was posture. Even in the forgetting, her body leaned forward, ready to act, ready to insist that this moment matters.

Presence and posture are two languages that outlast words.

I have learned to measure my own life that way. Not by how many statements I have crafted, but by how many people felt steadier after hearing them. Not by how many times I have been quoted, but by how often my silence made space for someone else to speak. The work is not only to be heard. The work is to be helpful.

If this book began with a flood of noise and the failure of leadership, let it end with the ache and the beauty of quiet. The quiet in a hospital room where monitors blink and you bargain with God for another sunrise. The quiet in a city that waits too long to be told the truth. The quiet in a grandmother's house where language grows thin and love grows loud.

Silence can be a sanctuary. It can also be a surrender. Leaders must learn the difference.

So here is my final request to every communicator, every CEO, every pastor, principal, organizer, and public servant who has made it to this page. Do not wait for history to hand you a microphone. Practice now. Do not wait for certainty to choose clarity. Speak now. Do not wait for unanimous approval to tell an honest truth. Lead now.

Speak in a way that feeds people first. Speak in a way that fights for them next. Then speak again tomorrow, so the rhythm becomes reliable and trust becomes unshakeable.

Tell the truth even when it trembles. Name the harm even when it hurts. Show the plan even when it is imperfect. Return with updates even when the cameras are gone.

That is how messages become movements. That is how voices become vows.

I think often of the last time Roxie's words narrowed to two. She sat by the window, nodding to a melody only she could hear. I blessed the food the way she once taught me to, simple and sincere, and when I finished she lifted her chin and answered the way she always had. "Jesus wept." It was not a resignation. It was an invitation. A reminder that the most powerful leader the world has ever known did not avoid grief or hide from truth. He entered it, named it, and drew near. If that is the model, then the work of communication is not performance. It is presence. It is permission for people to feel what they feel and still find the courage to move forward.

Ida taught me to feed with faith, and Roxie taught me to act with urgency. Together, they taught me to keep speaking, especially when silence would be easier. They taught me that voice is not about volume, but about responsibility, and that the truest leadership often sounds like care delivered on time.

So to you, the steward of someone's trust and the author of somebody's calm, make a promise with me here at the end. Use your voice to make people feel seen. Use your words to make people feel safe. Use your cadence to make people feel sure. And when you are gone, let it be said that you repeated your values so faithfully that they continued speaking without you.

If not now, then when. If not you, then who. If not with love, then why. Go feed. Go fight. Go speak. And whatever storm comes next, do not let the message break before the levee does.

Acknowledgments

Writing this book has been one of the most humbling and transformative experiences of my life. It is more than a collection of lessons on communication and leadership. It is a reflection of the people who shaped me, challenged me, and believed in me when I needed it most.

First and foremost, I thank God for the grace and strength that carried me through every page. Every insight and every story in this book was guided by something greater than myself.

To my children, Ahmad, Mark Alan, Mya Roxie, London Doris, and DeShawn, you are my greatest teachers. You have shown me the power of patience, resilience, and unconditional love. Every late night and early morning that went into this project was fueled by the desire to create something that would make you proud. You are my purpose, and you are my proof that love and legacy can coexist.

To my family, thank you for the foundation you built beneath me. To my mother, Doris Smith, the person I most admire in the word, whose love and quiet strength have carried me through every chapter of my life. To my father, Clifford B. Smith, Jr., my biggest cheerleader and best friend, whose belief in me has never wavered and whose pride remains my constant motivation. To my little brother, Corey Smith, my best friend, strategist, and confidant, thank you for always listening, advising, and reminding me that I was built for this.

I am also deeply grateful for the women in my family who reinforced what my mother modeled every day. To my great aunt Joyce Cooper and my aunt Toni Williams, both educators and leaders, women of brilliance, beauty, and unmistakable presence. Through your lives, I witnessed what it looks like to build meaningful careers while nurturing family, to lead with confidence and intelligence, and to move through the world unapologetically accomplished. Even now, Aunt Joyce, at ninety-three and still sharp as ever, reminds me that purpose does not expire.

And to my grandmothers, Ida and Roxie, whose wisdom and faith still echo in every decision I make, thank you for teaching me that leadership begins at home with compassion, courage, and conviction.

With gratitude and love,
Dionna Smith
Atlanta, Georgia - 2026

About the Author

Dionna Smith is a nationally recognized communications strategist, author, and speaker known for helping leaders find the right words when it matters most. With more than two decades of experience across corporate, government, and political communications, she has built a career at the intersection of leadership, crisis, and storytelling. She is the creator of the **CALM™ leadership discipline**, which teaches leaders how to center themselves, acknowledge impact, lead with facts responsibly, and model accountability over time.

Having led communications in both corporate and government environments, Dionna has guided public leaders through high-stakes moments of national attention, including protests, public safety crises, natural disasters, and major economic and infrastructure initiatives. Her steady leadership, strategic clarity, and human-centered approach have positioned her as one of the most trusted voices in local government communications.

A sought-after spokesperson and speaker, Dionna has presented at national forums including SXSW and SHRM, and has served as a trusted policy advisor on federal and state education and technology policy. Her insights and leadership have been featured on national platforms including C-SPAN, NPR, Forbes, Fast Company, and CNN Money.

Before entering public service, Dionna held C-suite roles in the technology sector, where she led diversity, equity, and inclusion, government affairs, and corporate and executive communications during a period of heightened corporate accountability and social reckoning. Throughout her career, she has advised and worked alongside some of the world's most recognized brands, including Cisco, Delta Air Lines, LexisNexis, and Fiserv.

Her leadership and impact have been recognized with honors including the Leader of the Year Award from the American Consortium for Equity in Education and the Atlanta Business Chronicle's 40 Under 40.

Dionna attended Howard University and graduated from Tulane University, where she earned a degree in Media Arts. When she is not behind the podium or in the war room, she mentors emerging leaders, writes about leadership and authenticity, and enjoys traveling and live music. She and her family live in Atlanta.

On the Record: A Practical Guide to Crisis Communication for Executives and Public Leaders is her debut book.

Communicate clearly. Lead calmly. Stay present when it matters most.